LOW SALT
LOW SUGAR
LOW FAT
DESSERTS

Penny Ballantyne and Maureen Egan

A Nitty Gritty Cookbook

Printed in the United States of America.

ISBN 0-911954-89-9

Production Consultant:
   Vicki L. Crampton
Photographer: Kathryn Opp
Food Stylist:
   Carolyn Schirmacher Gerould
Illustrator: Carol Webb Atherly
Back Cover Photography: Don Kerkhof

   For their cooperation in sharing props and locations for use in photographs, we extend special thanks to Zell Brothers Jewelers.

Table of Contents

Introduction

We love desserts! As wives and mothers, we take great pleasure in making nutritious, tasty desserts for our families. It's a way to show we care. We know that people today are concerned about the dangers of a high calorie, high fat diet and the resultant health problems. In our ten years of experimenting with recipes, we have developed many delicious low calorie, low fat desserts that fit into a prudent diet. Our easy-to-follow recipes are healthful modifications of traditional American favorites. Each recipe lists the amount of calories, carbohydrates, fats saturated and unsaturated, cholesterol and sodium per serving. We have formulated these recipes into this seasonal dessert cookbook. We include a chapter with guidelines for modifying both old favorites and new recipes. This cookbook will appeal to those who want to change the way they eat, but not give up their familiar desserts.

Seasonal Theme

Many of us are beginning to realize that our lifestyles have insulated us from the natural world and its seasonal rhythms. We live and work in artificially lighted, heated and cooled environments. Instant meals are available in restaurants and frozen food departments of supermarkets. Because of the availability of imported fresh produce year round, just about any food is available in any season. We pay a premium for this luxury, both monetarily and in the quality of our lives.

It isn't necessary to discard your lifestyle in order to get back in touch with the seasons. You can start by making small changes, like preparing a wonderful recipe using seasonal, fresh ingredients. Who doesn't look forward to the spring after a cold, wet winter? Or the cooler evenings and harvest time of autumn after hot summer days? By focusing your eating with the seasons, you refocus your self and your family.

Calculating Fat Calories

It is recommended that no more than 20% of your daily calories be from fat. Of that 20%, two-thirds should be polyunsaturated and one third saturated fat. But how do you figure it out? Let's say your daily caloric intake is 1500 calories. Multiply the number of calories (1500) by .2 (20% fat) to give you the number of fat calories per day. In this case it would be 1500 x .2 = 300 fat calories. Now take the number of fat calories and divide by 9 (9 calories per 1 gram of fat) to give you the total number of grams of fat per day, or, 300 ÷ 9 = 33.3 grams of fat.

If you know your daily caloric intake (1800 calories) and the number of grams of fat (40 grams), but want to find out what percent of your calories are from fat, use this formula: the number of grams of fat (40 grams) times 9 (9 calories per 1 gram of fat) divided by the total calories (1800 calories) times 100 equals the percent of calories you obtain from fat: $40 \times 9 = 360 \div 1800 = .2 \times 100 = 20\%$.

All the recipes in this book contain less than 200 calories and less than 7 grams of fat per serving. Each of the recipes lists the nutritional content to help you calculate your daily requirements. In choosing a dessert, keep in mind what you've already eaten for breakfast, lunch and dinner. If your previous meals and snacks were relatively high in calories and fat, choose a dessert that is lower in calories and fat. On the other hand, if your meals were not high in calories and fat, you can pick a dessert that is a little higher in calories and fat. These are all just guidelines to help you make intelligent decisions about the foods you eat.

List of Ingredients

Flours and Grains

It is a good idea that half the flour you bake with is whole wheat flour. Whole wheat pastry flour works best, as it is milled from soft wheat berries. This makes for a finer textured flour that produces less gluten when mixed, resulting in a more tender dessert. Other good flours to use are unbleached white flour and rye flour. For added fiber, incorporate oat and wheat bran, along with rolled oats. If you feel like experimenting, these flours can be interchanged for some interesting textures and flavors.

Sweeteners

Many people love desserts. Keeping it under control is a big challenge. The recipes in this book cut the amounts of sweeteners substantially while still maintaining a sweet taste. Honey can be used in some recipes to produce the same sweetness as sugar. Frozen unsweetened fruit juice concentrates are other sweeteners which can be used in baking. In general, sweeteners are empty calorie foods that need to be used sparingly.

Fats

The only fats recommended are vegetable oils and unsalted margarine. Butter is a total saturated fat. If you decide to use it for part or all of the fat in these recipes, be aware that you are changing the ratio of saturated to unsaturated fat. As fats are twice as high in calories gram for gram as proteins and carbohydrates, reducing the fat in desserts is an effective way to cut down on calories.

Fruits, Vegetables, Nuts

By using fresh fruits and vegetables in desserts, you not only enhance the flavor and appearance of your desserts, but give them a nutritional boost as well. Shop in your local markets to find the freshest produce in season. Nuts are very high in calories and fat, although the fat is unsaturated. If used sparingly, nuts lend a nice crunch and taste to desserts. If you have a favorite kind, by all means substitute it in place of what is listed.

Eggs

Eggs are a wonderful source of protein, but unfortunately the yolk is a major source of cholesterol. That's why two egg whites are substituted for one whole egg in most recipes. In certain desserts where the yolk is essential, as in a spongecake, the number of whole eggs is reduced and the remaining eggs are replaced with egg whites. There are a number of excellent egg substitutes on the market which can be used interchangeably.

Dairy

Skim or 1% butterfat milk is lower in fat and calories than whole milk. Buttermilk gives as tender a texture as butter would to desserts, without the added fat and calories. Since cream is loaded with saturated fat and calories it is never recommended. Instead, whipped ricotta cheese, buttermilk, or lightly sweetened lowfat yogurt will give the same creaminess to a dessert.

General Guidelines For Baking

Pies and Pastries

Most of the calories and fat in pies and pastries are found in the crust. A typical 9" two-crust pie made with shortening that serves eight, has 266 calories and 19 grams of fat per serving. That doesn't include the filling! A way to reduce those numbers is to use a single crust or cut smaller servings. And use the various recipes in this book which are slimmed down versions that average 130 calories and 7 grams of fat. Another way to avoid high amounts of fats but still have a flaky pastry is to use filo dough. The paper-thin sheets are naturally flaky, and by reducing the fat used to brush the dough with, you can make excellent pastries that are low in fat and calories. Making fruit pies and pastries is a great way to get more fiber in your diet. You can substitute any of your favorite local fruits in these recipes.

Cakes, Fillings, Icings

Cakes and icings are a challenge to make with reduced amounts of sugar and fat. But cakes are popular and these recipes are very tasty. Without much fat in the batter, these cakes have a tendency to stick to the pans. To solve this problem, lightly grease the pan. Then cut out the pan shape from waxed paper and place it in the pan before pouring in the batter. After cooling the cake for ten minutes, invert and peel off the paper. If a cake is to be split in half, freeze it first to make it firmer and easier to slice.

Cookies and Bars

Everyone loves cookies, especially kids. The recipes in this book are easy for kids to follow and help make. To help with the clean-up, use parchment paper to line the cookie sheets. After you are finished baking, the mess is on the paper, not the pan. Parchment paper can be found in your local grocery store or kitchenwares stores.

Spring

The birds are back; it's spring! Time to move the exercise program and seedlings outdoors! When the weather turns warm and you shed your winter woolens, the excesses of winter are obvious to all. Now's the time to lighten up your body and your menus. Jog through the park, join friends for a set of tennis, and take week-end bike rides with your family.

If you, too, become more active in spring, you'll want to compliment your fitness program by eating lighter and healthier meals. It's easy to do with all the fresh, new produce in the markets. Delicious desserts can be a snap to make by using seasonal ingredients. Citrus fruits — oranges, lemons, limes — are still in abundance and provide a light, tangy flavor as well as vitamin C. The earliest harvest from your garden is rhubarb. It's great combined with the season's first juicy strawberries. The taste of fresh pineapple is worth the extra time it takes to prepare. Fresh pineapple filling is delicious between feather-light cake layers. In some parts of the country it's maple sugar time. Pure maple syrup lends a wonderful flavor to puddings, cookies and even light frostings.

Many spring occasions call for a more festive dessert. You need not rely on heavy, fattening decorations. Fresh fruit and flowers can change an everyday dessert into an elegant finale.

Spring

Banana Orange Tart

This beautiful tart is almost too pretty to eat. But go ahead; it tastes as good as it looks.

Crust:
½ cup whole wheat pastry flour
½ cup unbleached white flour
3 tbs. unsalted margarine
3 tbs. cold water

Combine flours. Cut in margarine. Add only enough water to form a dough. Roll dough out on a floured piece of waxed paper. Fit into a lightly greased 11" x 7" tart pan with removable bottom. Prick all over with a fork. Bake at 375° for 15 minutes. Cool.

Filling:
1 medium banana
½ cup sugarless orange marmalade or apricot jam

Puree both in a food processor or blender.

Tart:
¼ cup sugarless orange marmalade or apricot jam
1 tsp. water
3 medium bananas, thinly sliced
3 navel oranges, peel and white membrane removed, thinly sliced

Bring marmalade and water to a boil. Strain. Glaze bottom of baked shell. Spread filling over bottom. Place a row of sliced bananas lengthwise down one side of filling. Arrange a row of sliced oranges next to bananas, then another row of bananas, then oranges, then bananas. Brush fruit with remaining glaze, reheating if necessary. Chill before serving.

Nutritional information per serving Calories 143; Protein grams 2; Carbohydrate grams 33; Total fat grams 3; Saturated fat grams .4; Unsaturated fat grams 2.6; Cholesterol 0 mg; Sodium 0 mg

Strawberry Tartlets

Servings: 8

Just the dessert to make with those first June berries.

Crust:
½ cup whole wheat pastry flour

½ cup unbleached white flour

3 tbs. unsalted margarine

3-4 tbs. cold water

Combine flours. Cut in margarine. Add only enough water to hold dough together. Roll out on a floured piece of waxed paper. Cut 8 circles to fit into 8 3" tart shells. Prick dough all over with a fork. Bake at 375° for 10-12 minutes until shells are light brown. Cool before filling.

Filling:
1 quart fresh strawberries, mashed

½ cup sugar

3 tbs. cornstarch

1 pint fresh strawberries, sliced

In a saucepan, combine mashed strawberries, sugar and cornstarch. Bring to a boil, stirring. Boil over medium heat one minute, until mixture thickens, stirring constantly. Cool. Spoon into prepared tartlet shells. Top with sliced strawberries. Cover with plastic wrap and chill before serving.

Nutritional information per serving Calories 193; Protein grams 3; Carbohydrate grams 37; Total fat grams 5; Saturated fat grams .8; Unsaturated fat grams 4.2; Cholesterol 0 mg; Sodium 0 mg

Strawberry Rhubarb Cobbler

Low in fat doesn't mean low on flavor. Here's a scaled down version of an old family favorite.

3 tbs. cornstarch
⅔ cup sugar

4 cups rhubarb cut in ½" pieces
1 cup sliced fresh strawberries

Combine sugar and cornstarch. Mix together with rhubarb and strawberries. Pour into a lightly greased 11" x 7" pan. Bake at 400° for 5 minutes while biscuit topping is prepared.

Biscuit Topping:

½ cup whole wheat pastry flour
½ cup unbleached white flour
1 tbs. sugar

1-1½ tsp. baking powder
3 tbs. unsalted margarine
½ cup skim milk

Combine flours, sugar and baking powder. Cut in margarine. Add milk and mix until dough forms a ball. Remove fruit from oven. Spoon eight mounds of dough on top of fruit. Bake for 25 to 30 minutes until biscuits are browned.

Nutritional information per serving Calories 190; Protein grams 3; Carbohydrate grams 36; Total fat grams 5; Saturated fat grams .7; Unsaturated fat grams 4.3; Cholesterol 0 mg; Sodium 87 mg

---

Bananas in Pastry

A unique dessert that will bring raves.

½ cup whole wheat pastry flour
½ cup unbleached white flour
3 tbs. unsalted margarine

3 tbs. cold water
5 small bananas, peeled

Combine flours. Cut in margarine. Add only enough water to form a dough. Divide dough into 5 equal pieces. Roll a piece into a rectangle slightly longer and twice as wide as banana. Place banana in center and pinch sides and ends to enclose banana. Prick in several places with a fork. Place on a lightly greased cookie sheet. Repeat with remaining dough and bananas. Bake at 400° for 15 minutes until crust is browned. Serve warm with sauce.

Sauce:

½ cup plain lowfat yogurt
1 tbs. honey

Beat honey into yogurt until smooth.

Nutritional information per serving Calories 195; Protein grams 4; Carbohydrate grams 42; Total fat grams 7; Saturated fat grams 1.1; Unsaturated fat grams 5.9; Cholesterol 0 mg; Sodium 17 mg

Fresh Rhubarb Pie

The small amount of honey used allows the tartness of the rhubarb to come through. Be ready to pucker up when you bite into this pie!

Crust:
¾ cup whole wheat pastry flour
¾ cup unbleached white flour

4½ tbs. unsalted margarine
5-6 tbs. cold water

Combine flours. Cut in margarine. Add only enough water to form a dough. Roll out ⅔ of dough on a floured piece of waxed paper. Put in a 9" lightly greased pie pan. Roll out remaining dough with the scraps. Cut into 8 strips.

Filling:
5 cups chopped rhubarb (½" pieces)
½ cup unbleached white flour
½ cup honey

Toss rhubarb with flour. Add honey and mix well. Spoon filling into prepared crust. Place 4 strips across filling. Brush with water. Arrange other 4 strips diagonally across first strips. Brush with water. Bake at 375° for 40 minutes until filling is bubbly and crust is browned.

Nutritional information per serving Calories 197; Protein grams 3; Carbohydrate grams 36; Total fat grams 6; Saturated fat grams 1.2; Unsaturated fat grams 4.8; Cholesterol 0 mg; Sodium 0 mg

---

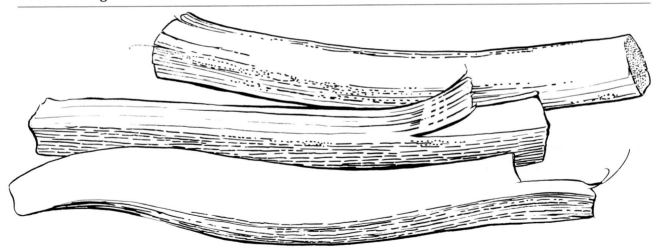

Orange Chiffon Pie

This is a wonderfully light pie with the tangy taste of oranges.

Crust:
1 cup graham cracker crumbs
1 tbs. unsalted margarine, melted

Combine crumbs and margarine. Press into a lightly greased 9" pie pan. Bake at 375° for 5 to 7 minutes. Cool before filling.

Filling:
2 envelopes unflavored gelatin
1 cup cold water
6 ozs. unsweetened orange concentrate, thawed
¼ cup honey

2 cups plain lowfat yogurt
3 egg whites
1 tbs. honey
orange slices

Soften gelatin in water. Cook over low heat until gelatin is dissolved. Set aside. Combine juice concentrate, ¼ cup honey and yogurt. Whisk in gelatin. Chill until almost set, about one hour. Whip whites to soft peaks. Add honey and whip to firm peaks. Fold whites into yogurt-orange mixture. Pour into prepared pie shell. Chill several hours until firm. Garnish with orange slices before serving.

Nutritional information per serving Calories 147; Protein grams 5; Carbohydrate grams 34; Total fat grams 3; Saturated fat grams .6; Unsaturated fat grams 2.4; Cholesterol 3 mg; Sodium 84 mg

Lemon Chiffon Pie

Make this with lime instead of lemon for a refreshing change.

Crust:
1¼ cups graham cracker crumbs
1 tbs. unsalted margarine, melted

Combine crumbs and margarine. Press into a lightly greased 9" pie pan. Bake at 375° for 5 to 7 minutes. Cool before filling.

Filling:
¼ cup water
1 envelope **plus** 1 tsp. unflavored gelatin
⅓ cup sugar
¼ cup water
3 egg yolks
¼ cup lemon juice

2 tsp. grated lemon peel
3 egg whites
¼ tsp. cream of tartar
⅓ cup sugar
lemon slices

Soften gelatin in ¼ cup water. Mix together ⅓ cup sugar, ¼ cup water, egg yolks and lemon juice. Add to softened gelatin. Cook over low heat until mixture thickens slightly. Stir in lemon peel. Chill until mixture begins to set. Whip egg whites until frothy. Add cream of tartar and whip to soft peaks. Add sugar slowly and whip to firm peaks. Fold into lemon mixture. Spoon into prepared crust. Chill 4 hours or overnight. Before serving, garnish with lemon slices.

Nutritional information per serving   Calories 151; Protein grams 4; Carbohydrate grams 24; Total fat grams 5; Saturated fat grams .8; Unsaturated fat grams 4.2; Cholesterol 102 mg; Sodium 26 mg

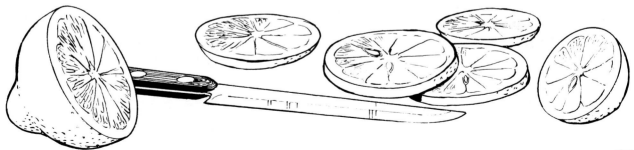

Rhubarb Cake

This is an adaptation of a family favorite, Ruth's Rhubarb Cake. Even Ruth couldn't tell the difference!

⅓ cup unsalted margarine
½ cup brown sugar
½ cup white sugar
1 egg
1 tsp. vanilla
1 tsp. baking soda

1 cup buttermilk
2 cups unbleached white flour
2 cups rhubarb, cut in ½" pieces
⅓ cup sugar
¾ tsp. cinnamon

Cream margarine, ½ cup brown sugar and ½ cup white sugar until light. Beat in egg and vanilla. Stir baking soda into buttermilk. Alternately add buttermilk and flour to creamed mixture. Fold in rhubarb. Pour into a lightly greased 9" x 13" pan. Combine ⅓ cup sugar and cinnamon. Sprinkle over batter before baking. Bake at 375° for 30 minutes. Cool.

Nutritional information per serving Calories 160; Protein grams 3; Carbohydrate grams 23; Total fat grams 4; Saturated fat grams .7; Unsaturated fat grams 3.3; Cholesterol 17 mg; Sodium 72 mg

Pineapple-filled Cake

This is a lovely spring cake. Fresh pineapple filling takes the place of heavy frosting.

2 layers of basic white cake
fresh pineapple slices
Filling:

1 tbs. sugar
3 tbs. cornstarch

1 cup chopped fresh pineapple, drained
2 tsp. grated lemon rind

Combine sugar and cornstarch in a saucepan. Add pineapple and lemon rind. Cook until mixture is thickened and transparent, stirring constantly. If too thick, thin with pineapple juice.

Assembly: Place one cake layer on serving plate. Spread with half of filling. Place second layer on top of first. Spread with remaining filling. Arrange pineapple slices on top.

Nutritional information per serving Calories 171; Protein grams 3; Carbohydrate grams 30; Total fat grams 5; Saturated fat grams .3; Unsaturated fat grams 4.7; Cholesterol 0 mg; Sodium 130 mg

Maple Chiffon Cake

Sugaring time in the spring is a good time to celebrate with some of the season's first maple syrup.

2 cups unbleached white flour
2 tbs. cornstarch
1 tbs. baking powder
¾ cup brown sugar
⅓ cup vegetable oil

4 egg yolks
½ cup pure maple syrup
⅔ cup water
1 cup egg whites (about 7)
½ tsp. cream of tartar

Sift flour, cornstarch and baking powder. Set aside. Mix together brown sugar, oil, egg yolks, maple syrup and water. Stir this into dry ingredients and beat until smooth. Whip egg whites with cream of tartar to firm peaks. Fold whites into batter until just blended. Pour into a 10" ungreased tube pan. Bake at 325° for 45 minutes until top appears dry and springs back when touched. Invert to cool. Remove when cooled and glaze.

Maple glaze:

⅔ cup powdered sugar
3 tbs. pure maple syrup, warmed

Beat ingredients until smooth. Drizzle over cake.

Nutritional information per serving   Calories 196; Protein grams 4; Carbohydrate grams 31; Total fat grams 6; Saturated fat grams .7; Unsaturated fat grams 5.3; Cholesterol 68 mg; Sodium 109 mg

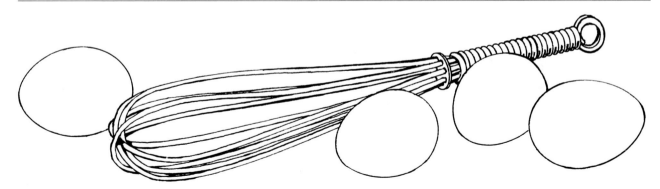

Farina Cheesecake

Farina isn't just for breakfast. Try this delicious cheesecake for a tasty surprise!

Crust:
¾ cup crushed sugarless cereal flakes
1½ tbs. unsalted margarine

Combine crushed cereal flakes and margarine. Press into bottom of a lightly greased 8" springform pan. Bake at 375° for 5 minutes. Cool.

Filling:
1 serving of cooled Cream of Wheat (2½ tbs. Cream of Wheat cooked with
    1 cup skim milk until thick)
8 ozs. neufchatel cheese, room temperature
¼ cup honey
2 eggs
2 tsp. vanilla
2 tsp. lemon juice

Beat neufchatel cheese and honey until light. Stir in remaining ingredients and cooled Cream of Wheat cereal. Pour into prepared crust. Bake at 325° for 40 minutes until set. Cool, and then refrigerate. Before serving, top with fresh fruit.

Nutritional information per serving   Calories 130; Protein grams 4; Carbohydrate grams 10; Total fat grams 7; Saturated fat grams 3; Unsaturated fat grams 4; Cholesterol 55 mg; Sodium 104 mg

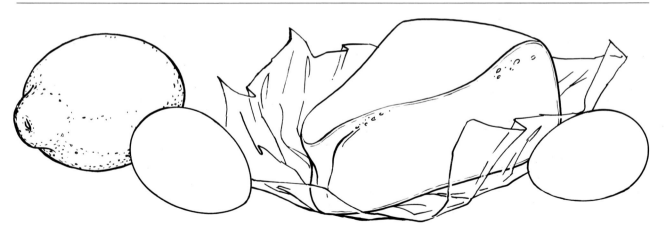

Basic White Cake

You can decorate this versatile cake to fit any occasion.

1⅓ cups unbleached white flour
2 tsp. baking powder
½ tsp. baking soda
½ cup sugar
¼ cup vegetable oil

2 tsp. vanilla
1 cup buttermilk
3 egg whites
¼ tsp. cream of tartar
⅓ cup sugar

Sift dry ingredients. Combine oil, vanilla and buttermilk. Stir into dry ingredients. Whip egg whites until foamy. Add cream of tartar and whip to soft peaks. Add ⅓ cup sugar slowly and whip to firm peaks. Fold whites into batter. Pour into two 8″ cake pans, lightly greased and with a waxed paper circle on the bottom. Bake at 350° for 20 minutes. Invert layers onto rack to cool. Remove waxed paper.

Nutritional information per serving Calories 146; Protein grams 3; Carbohydrate grams 24; Total fat grams 5; Saturated fat grams .3; Unsaturated fat grams 4.7; Cholesterol 0 mg; Sodium 130 mg

Banana Orange Tart (page 10) ▶

Decorated Party Cake

Here is just one way to dress up Basic White Cake.

2 layers of basic white cake
6 tbs. sugarless jam
Icing:
½ cup sugar
¼ cup water

2 egg whites
¼ tsp. cream of tartar

Bring water and sugar to a boil. Cook to 240° or soft ball stage. Don't burn! Whip egg whites with cream of tartar to soft peaks. Slowly pour in hot sugar syrup. Whip to firm peaks.

Assembly: Place one cake layer on serving plate. Spread top with 3 tbs. jam. Place second layer on top of first. Spread top with remaining 3 tbs. jam. Frost sides of cake with icing. Pipe a shell border around top and bottom edge and place fresh flowers on top, if desired.

Nutritional information per serving Calories 198; Protein grams 3; Carbohydrate grams 26; Total fat grams 5; Saturated fat grams .3; Unsaturated fat grams 4.7; Cholesterol 0 mg; Sodium 144 mg

Ginger Crisps

These spicy, light wafers go well with lemon or lime sherbet.

1¼ cups unbleached white flour
1 cup whole wheat pastry flour
½ tsp. baking soda
1½ tsp. ginger
½ tsp. **each** cinnamon, nutmeg,
   cloves, allspice

⅓ cup sugar
¾ cup molasses
¼ cup unsalted margarine
1 egg

Combine dry ingredients. Set aside. Cream sugar, molasses and margarine. Beat in egg. Add dry ingredients. Drop dough by rounded teaspoons onto lightly greased cookie sheets. Flatten cookies with back of spoon or fingers. Bake at 350° for 8 to 10 minutes. Cool.

Nutritional information per cookie Calories 31; Protein grams 0; Carbohydrate grams 6; Total fat grams 1; Saturated fat grams .1; Unsaturated fat grams .9; Cholesterol 4 mg; Sodium 7 mg

Strawberry Teacakes

Serve these bite-sized sandwich cookies at teatime or any time.

⅓ cup unsalted margarine
⅓ cup sugar
2 egg whites
1 tsp. vanilla
¾ cup whole wheat pastry flour

¾ cup unbleached white flour
1 tsp. baking powder
¼ cup sugarless jam
powdered sugar

Cream margarine and sugar. Beat in egg whites and vanilla. Stir in flours and baking powder. Chill dough. Roll out ⅛" thick on floured surface. Cut out sixty 2" circles. In 30 of them, cut a small circle out of middle. Bake on a lightly greased cookie sheet at 350° for 7 minutes. Cool. Spread a thin layer of jam on bottom whole circles. Dust cookies that have a hole in the middle with powdered sugar. Sandwich together.

Nutritional information per cookie   Calories 54; Protein grams 1; Carbohydrate grams 11; Total fat grams 2; Saturated fat grams .3; Unsaturated fat grams 1.7; Cholesterol 0 mg; Sodium 18 mg

---

Lady Fingers

Versatile and tasty, lady fingers are easy and fun to make.

1 egg
½ cup sugar
1 tsp. vanilla
3 egg whites

1 tbs. sugar
⅔ cup unbleached flour, sifted
powdered sugar

Whip egg with ½ cup sugar and vanilla until thick and pale yellow. In another bowl, whip egg whites to soft peaks. Add 1 tbs. sugar slowly and whip to firm peaks. Alternately fold egg whites and flour into the yolk mixture. Gently spoon batter into a pastry bag fitted with a ½" plain opening. Lightly grease two cookie sheets, or line with parchment paper. Squeeze out batter into 4" x 1½" fingers, one inch apart on sheets. Lightly dust fingers with powdered sugar. Bake at 300° for 20 minutes until light tan. Fingers should be crisp on the outside and soft inside. Cool.

Nutritional information per cookie Calories 23; Protein grams 1; Carbohydrate grams 5; Total fat grams 0; Saturated fat grams 0; Unsaturated fat grams 0; Cholesterol 10 mg; Sodium 8 mg

Strawberry Bars

These bars are something different to make when you tire of the usual strawberry desserts.

½ cup whole wheat pastry flour
¼ cup unbleached white flour
¼ tsp. baking soda
¼ tsp. cinnamon
¼ cup honey
1 egg
¼ cup vegetable oil
½ cup sliced strawberries, slightly mashed

Combine flours, soda and cinnamon. Combine honey, egg and oil and add to dry ingredients. Stir in strawberries. Pour into a lightly greased 8" x 8" pan. Bake at 350° for 20 minutes.

Nutritional information per bar   Calories 92; Protein grams 1; Carbohydrate grams 16; Total fat grams 5; Saturated fat grams .2; Unsaturated fat grams 4.8; Cholesterol 23 mg; Sodium 6 mg

---

Grandma's Date-filled Cookies

These are one of Grandma's specialties, adapted to be lower in fat and calories, but with the same great taste. Uncle Sharky loves them!

Filling:
1 cup chopped dates
¼ cup apple juice
2 tbs. water

Cook dates with juice and water until dates are very soft. Add more water, if necessary. Cool before using.

Cookie Dough:
½ cup brown sugar
¼ cup unsalted margarine
1 egg white
1 tsp. baking powder

¾ cup whole wheat pastry flour
¾ cup unbleached white flour
skim milk

Cream brown sugar, margarine and egg white. Stir in flours and baking powder. Chill dough several hours or overnight. Roll out dough ⅛" on floured surface. Cut thirty-six 3" circles. On half the circles, cut a 1" circle out of middle. Place a teaspoon of date filling on the cookies without the hole. Brush edges with skim milk. Place the cookies with the hole on top of each. Press edges together. Bake at 350° for 12 minutes.

Nutritional information per cookie Calories 103; Protein grams 1; Carbohydrate grams 17; Total fat grams 3; Saturated fat grams .5; Unsaturated fat grams 2.5; Cholesterol 0 mg; Sodium 18 mg

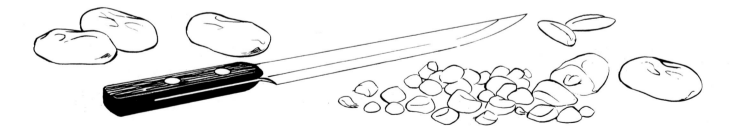

Lemon Bars

A melt-in-your-mouth lemony bar.

Filling:
⅔ cup water
2½ tbs. cornstarch
3 tbs. sugar
3 tbs. lemon juice
2 tsp. lemon peel

In a saucepan, dissolve cornstarch and sugar in water. Add lemon juice and cook over medium heat until thickened, stirring constantly. Remove from heat and add lemon peel. Cool slightly before using.

Streusel:
⅓ cup whole wheat pastry flour
⅓ cup unbleached white flour
1 cup quick oats
¼ cup sugar

3 tbs. unsalted margarine
2 tbs. unsweetened apple juice
    concentrate, thawed
powdered sugar (optional)

Combine flours, oats and sugar. Cut in margarine. Add juice and stir to coat mixture. Don't overmix. Press half the mixture firmly into a lightly greased 8" x 8" pan. Carefully spread lemon filling over bottom. Sprinkle rest of streusel over filling. Press streusel lightly. Bake at 350° for 20 minutes. Cool completely before cutting into bars. Dust lightly with powdered sugar if desired.

Nutritional information per bar   Calories 107; Protein grams 1; Carbohydrate grams 8; Total fat grams 3; Saturated fat grams .4; Unsaturated fat grams 2.6; Cholesterol 0 mg; Sodium 1 mg

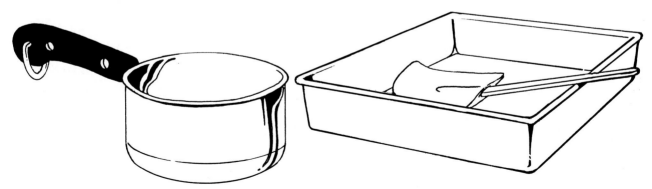

Hermits

We never picnic at the beach without our hermits. These wonderful bars travel well. Take them with you on your next outing.

⅓ cup unsalted margarine
⅔ cup sugar
1 tsp. baking soda
¼ tsp. cinnamon
1 tbs. molasses
1 egg

1 cup whole wheat pastry flour
¾ cup unbleached white flour
2 tbs. **plus** 1 tsp. water
½ cup raisins
skim milk

Cream the first five ingredients. Beat in egg. Stir in remaining ingredients until well blended. Divide dough in half. On a floured surface, roll each half into a long cylinder. Place each cylinder lengthwise on a lightly greased cookie sheet. Press flat. Brush with skim milk. Bake at 350° for 10 to 12 minutes. Glaze while bars are warm. Cut each strip into 12 bars.

Glaze:

¼ cup powdered sugar
½ tsp. vanilla
1 tsp. skim milk

Beat all ingredients until smooth.

Nutritional information per bar   Calories 98; Protein grams 1; Carbohydrate grams 19; Total fat grams 3; Saturated fat grams .5; Unsaturated fat grams 2.5; Cholesterol 11 mg; Sodium 37 mg

Sugar-free Oatmeal Raisin Cookies

16 cookies

A delicious cookie sweetened only with fruit juice concentrates. Kids love them!

1 cup quick oats
⅓ cup whole wheat pastry flour
¼ tsp. baking soda
¼ tsp. cinnamon
2 tbs. raisins
¼ cup unsweetened pineapple juice concentrate, thawed
¼ cup unsweetened apple juice concentrate, thawed
¼ cup vegetable oil

Combine dry ingredients and raisins. Stir in juice concentrates and oil. Drop by teaspoons onto a lightly greased cookie sheet. Bake at 350° for 10 minutes.

Nutritional information per cookie Calories 66; Protein grams 1; Carbohydrate grams 7; Total fat grams 3; Saturated fat grams .2; Unsaturated fat grams 2.8; Cholesterol 0 mg; Sodium 14 mg

Bananas Flambé

This is an impressive finale to a special dinner. Turn out the lights before igniting the rum.

3 large bananas, halved lengthwise and quartered
1 tbs. unsalted margarine
2 tbs. brown sugar
¾ cup unsweetened pineapple juice
¼ tsp. cinnamon
¼ cup rum
1 quart vanilla ice milk (optional)

In a skillet, melt margarine. Add brown sugar, pineapple juice, cinnamon and bananas. Cook over medium heat until bananas begin to soften, basting often. In a saucepan, warm rum. Pour over bananas and ignite. When the flames are out, stir and serve over ice milk. Or serve bananas in a dessert dish.

Nutritional information per serving Calories 93; Protein grams 0; Carbohydrate grams 16; Total fat grams 2; Saturated fat grams .1; Unsaturated fat grams 1.9; Cholesterol 0 mg; Sodium 55 mg

Rhubarb Compote

Apples add a new twist to this seasonal favorite.

1 pound rhubarb, cut into 1" pieces
3 medium apples, peeled, cored and cut into 8ths
¼ tsp. cinnamon
¼ tsp. grated lemon peel
⅓ cup sugar
¼ cup unsweetened apple juice concentrate

Combine all ingredients except juice concentrate. Let stand five minutes. Place fruit mixture in a saucepan with apple juice concentrate. Bring to a boil. Reduce heat and simmer, covered, until fruit is just tender. Spoon into 6 dessert dishes. Serve warm or chilled.

Nutritional information per serving Calories 115; Protein grams 0; Carbohydrate grams 29; Total fat grams 0; Saturated fat grams 0; Unsaturated fat grams 0; Cholesterol 0 mg; Sodium 2 mg

---

Maple Pudding

For a delicious, decorative touch, sprinkle tops with pure maple sugar.

¼ cup pure maple syrup
1 tbs. brown sugar
1 tbs. cornstarch
1 egg

2 cups skim milk
1 tsp. vanilla
1 tbs. maple sugar

In a saucepan, beat all ingredients together except vanilla and maple sugar. Cook over medium heat, stirring constantly, until mixture boils and begins to thicken. Cook one minute more. Remove from heat and add vanilla. Spoon into 4 dessert dishes. While still warm, sprinkle maple sugar over tops. Serve warm, or chill before serving.

Nutritional information per serving Calories 143; Protein grams 6; Carbohydrate grams 27; Total fat grams 2; Saturated fat grams .5; Unsaturated fat grams 1.5; Cholesterol 70 mg; Sodium 85 mg

---

Fresh Strawberry Dessert

A quick and easy dessert that can be varied by adding other fruits.

3 tbs. unsweetened apple juice concentrate, thawed
2 tbs. water
1 envelope **plus** 1 tsp. unflavored gelatin
2½ cups pureed strawberries
1 banana, sliced
3 tbs. lowfat ricotta cheese

Combine water and juice concentrate. Soften gelatin in mixture. Heat to dissolve. Heat mashed strawberries and stir in gelatin. Chill until partially set. Fold in sliced bananas. Spoon into 6 dessert glasses. Chill until firm. Before serving, top each with a teaspoon of ricotta cheese.

Nutritional information per serving Calories 68; Protein grams 3; Carbohydrate grams 12; Total fat grams 0; Saturated fat grams 0; Unsaturated fat grams 0; Cholesterol 2 mg; Sodium 10 mg

Maple Pudding (page 45) ▶

Summer

Our summer motto is, "in and out of the kitchen, fast!" so we make lots of cool garden salads, pasta with fresh vegetables and quick grilled lean meats. Even then, someone is sure to ask, "But what did you make for dessert?"

With the abundance of fresh produce from our gardens and markets, it is easy to create fresh, beautiful and healthy desserts with whatever we have on hand. By using these recipes as a guide, you can interchange the fruits and vegetables however you choose.

Some recipes call for cooked or pureed fruit. *Quick Blueberry Dessert* can also be made with raspberries. The *Jelly Roll* would be just as wonderful with strawberries. Any sugarless fruit jam can be substituted in the *Jam Bars.*

Many of these recipes use fresh fruit toppings. Blueberries could top the *Meringue Baskets* instead of raspberries. You can use any combination of fruits to top the *Fruit Flan, Yogurt Custard Tart, Strawberry Schaum Torte* or *Angelfood Cake.*

When you're in the mood for something frozen and frosty, make *Raspberry Ice* instead of *Blackberry Ice.* Try the *Cantaloupe Sherbet* with honeydew instead. Use any combination of berries you have on hand for the *Berry Ice Cream.* Make use of the summer's bounty and your imagination.

◀ **Orange Chiffon Pie (page 18) left, Lemon Chiffon Pie (page 20) top, Raspberry Chiffon Pie (page 52) right**

Summer

Yogurt-Custard Tart

A smooth filling that can be topped with an assortment of fresh fruit.

1 recipe crust to fit a 10″ pie or tart pan
   (see Fresh Fruit Tartlets or other pie recipes)
2 cups plain lowfat yogurt
¾ cup egg substitute or 1 whole egg **plus** 3 whites
½ cup sugar
¼ cup flour
1 tbs. vanilla
fresh fruit (strawberries, blueberries or raspberries)

Bake the pie crust in a preheated 375° oven for 10-12 minutes. Remove from oven and reduce heat to 350°.

In a large mixing bowl, mix all filling ingredients except fruit and pour into baked tart shell. Bake tart for 25-30 minutes or until the filling is set. Cool, top with fresh fruit, chill and serve.

Nutritional information per serving Calories 100; Protein grams 3; Carbohydrate grams 17; Total fat grams 1.6; Saturated fat grams 1; Unsaturated fat grams .6; Cholesterol 17 mg; Sodium 29.5 mg

Raspberry Chiffon Pie

Servings: 8

With the fresh taste of raspberries in a light chiffon cloud, it's easy to see why this is a favorite.

Crust:
1¼ cups graham cracker crumbs
1 tbs. unsalted margarine, melted

Combine crumbs and margarine. Press into a lightly greased 9" pie pan. Bake at 375° for 5 to 7 minutes. Cool before filling.

Filling:
3 cups fresh raspberries
¼ cup raspberry juice or water
1 envelope **plus** 1 tsp. unflavored gelatin
⅓ cup sugar

3 egg whites
¼ tsp. cream of tartar
⅓ cup sugar
1 cup plain lowfat yogurt

Mash raspberries, saving a few for garnish. Set aside. Soften gelatin in juice or water. Add ⅓ cup sugar. Heat to dissolve gelatin. Stir in mashed berries. Chill until mixture begins to set, about an hour. Whip egg whites until frothy. Add cream of tartar and whip to soft peaks. Add sugar slowly and whip to firm peaks. Fold into raspberry mixture. Fold in yogurt. Spoon into prepared crust. Chill 3 to 4 hours or overnight. Before serving, garnish with reserved raspberries.

Nutritional information per serving   Calories 167; Protein grams 5; Carbohydrate grams 29; Total fat grams 3; Saturated fat grams .3; Unsaturated fat grams 2.7; Cholesterol 0 mg; Sodium 22 mg

Fresh Fruit Tartlets

Servings: 8

These beautiful jewel-like treasures dress up a summer buffet table.

Crust:
½ cup whole wheat pastry flour
½ cup unbleached white flour

3 tbs. unsalted margarine
3-4 tbs. cold water

Combine flours. Cut in margarine. Add only enough water to hold dough together. Roll out on a floured piece of waxed paper. Cut 8 circles to fit into eight 3" tart shells. Prick dough all over with a fork. Bake at 375° for 10 to 12 minutes until shells are light brown. Cool before filling.

Filling:
1 cup lowfat ricotta cheese
2 tbs. sugar
1 tbs. lemon juice
½ tbs. grated lemon peel

½ tsp. vanilla
strawberries, cherries, raspberries, blueberries, grapes, melons, etc.
sugarless apricot jam

Combine all ingredients except fruit and jam and mix well. Fill prepared tart shells. Arrange fresh fruit on the tops in a pleasing manner. Glaze fruit with hot, strained apricot jam, if desired.

Nutritional information per serving Calories 125; Protein grams 5; Carbohydrate grams 15; Total fat grams 6; Saturated fat grams 1; Unsaturated fat grams 5; Cholesterol 4 mg; Sodium 20 mg

---

Yogurt Cream Cheese Pie

Servings: 12

This is a freezer pie that's rich and tangy. It can be served either straight from the freezer, or thawed slightly.

Crust:
1¼ cups graham cracker crumbs
1 tbs. unsalted margarine, melted

Combine crumbs and margarine. Press into a lightly greased 9" pie pan. Bake at 375° for 5 minutes. Cool before filling.

Filling:
2 tbs. cold water
2 tsp. unflavored gelatin
8 ozs. neufchatel cheese,
   room temperature
8 ozs. plain lowfat yogurt

⅓ cup honey
1 tsp. vanilla
2 cups sliced fresh fruit (peaches, strawberries, blueberries, etc.)

Soften gelatin in water. Heat to dissolve. Beat cheese until fluffy. Add yogurt, honey and vanilla. Beat until smooth. Stir in gelatin until well blended. Pour into prepared crust. Freeze pie until firm. Soften 10 minutes at room temperature and arrange fresh fruit on top before serving.

Nutritional information per serving   Calories 136; Protein grams 3; Carbohydrate grams 26; Total fat grams 6; Saturated fat grams 4.1; Unsaturated fat grams 1.9; Cholesterol 16 mg; Sodium 88 mg

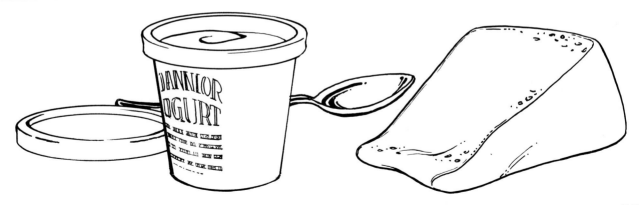

Fresh Cherry Pie

Be sure to use quick-cooking tapioca, not regular, and let the mixture stand the full fifteen minutes.

Crust:

¾ cup whole wheat pastry flour
¾ cup unbleached white flour

4½ tbs. unsalted margarine
4-5 tbs. cold water

Combine flours. Cut in margarine. Add only enough water to hold dough together. Roll out one-half of dough on a floured surface to fit an 8" pie pan. Place dough in pie pan. Brush edges with water. Spoon filling in. Roll out other half of dough. Place over filling. Seal top crust to bottom crust. Flute edges. Cut slits in top crust to allow steam to escape. Bake at 375° for 40 minutes.

Cherry Filling:

3 cups fresh pitted sour cherries
⅓ cup honey
2 tbs. cornstarch

2 tbs. quick-cooking tapioca
⅛ tsp. almond extract

Combine all ingredients and let stand 15 minutes. Stir and pour into prepared crust.

Nutritional information per serving   Calories 198; Protein grams 4; Carbohydrate grams 41; Total fat grams 7; Saturated fat grams 1; Unsaturated fat grams 6; Cholesterol 0 mg; Sodium 8 mg

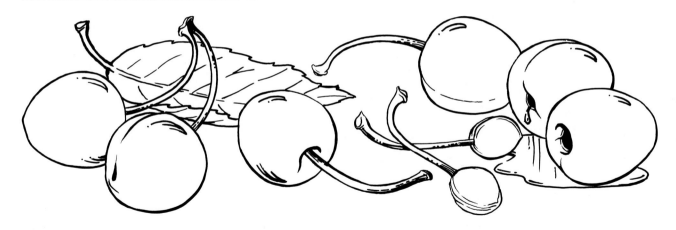

Fruit Flan

Make a colorful design on the top by alternating rows of contrasting colored fruit.

¼ cup unsalted margarine
⅓ cup sugar
2 tsp. vanilla
1 egg
2 egg whites
1⅓ cups unbleached flour

1½ tsp. baking powder
½ tsp. baking soda
⅔ cup buttermilk
½ cup sugarless jam
3 cups mixed fresh fruit, sliced

Cream margarine and sugar until light and fluffy. Beat in egg, egg whites and vanilla. Combine flour, baking powder and baking soda. Add to creamed mixture alternately with buttermilk. Spread into a 10″ lightly greased flan pan. Bake at 375° for 20 minutes until browned. Invert onto rack to cool. Spread cake with sugarless jam. Arrange fruit on top in a design.

Nutritional information per serving Calories 176; Protein grams 3; Carbohydrate grams 30; Total fat grams 4; Saturated fat grams .6; Unsaturated fat grams 3.4; Cholesterol 23 mg; Sodium 92 mg

Eggplant Cake

An unusual ingredient, eggplant, makes this cake moist and delicious.

1 medium eggplant, cooked and pureed
  (1 cup)
1 cup sugar
2 eggs **plus** 3 egg whites
½ cup oil
¾ cup buttermilk
1½ tsp. baking soda

¾ tsp. baking powder
1½ cups whole wheat flour
2 cups unbleached white flour
1 tsp. cinnamon
½ tsp. nutmeg
½ cup currants

Peel eggplant and cut it into cubes. Put the cubes into a saucepan of boiling water and cook until soft. Drain and puree eggplant in a food processor. In a large mixing bowl beat eggs, sugar, buttermilk and oil. Add 1 cup pureed eggplant, vanilla and currants. Sift flours, baking soda, baking powder, and spices. Add to the eggplant mixture and stir just until blended. Pour into a 10" bundt or tube pan which has been sprayed with nonstick cooking spray. Bake at 350° for 45 minutes or until cake tester comes out clean.

Nutritional information per serving Calories 152; Protein grams 16; Carbohydrate grams 12.9; Total fat grams 5.4; Saturated fat grams .6; Unsaturated fat grams 4.8; Cholesterol 21 mg; Sodium 42 mg

Cocoa Chiffon Cake

Cocoa adds rich chocolate flavor without adding fat.

2 eggs, separated
1¼ cups sugar
1¾ cups unbleached white flour
1 tbs. cornstarch

1 tsp. baking soda
⅓ cup oil
1 cup buttermilk
4 tbs. cocoa

Pans: two 8" round **or**
 one 9" x 13" **or**
 one 8" tube pan

In a small, deep mixing bowl, beat egg whites with electric beater until soft peaks form. Gradually add ½ cup of the sugar and continue beating until stiff peaks form and whites are glossy. Set aside.

Into a large mixing bowl, sift flour, cornstarch, cocoa, baking soda, and remaining sugar. Add oil and ½ cup buttermilk. Beat on high one minute. Add yolks, sugar and remaining buttermilk. Beat one more minute. Scrape bowl and stir in ½ cup meringue. Fold in the rest of the meringue. Pour into pans which have been sprayed with nonstick cooking spray. Bake at 350° for 30 minutes or until cake tester comes out clean. Cool on wire rack.

Nutritional information per serving Calories 171; Protein grams 9; Carbohydrate grams 35; Total fat grams 7; Saturated fat grams 1.6; Unsaturated fat grams 5.4; Cholesterol 42 mg; Sodium 101 mg

Chocolate Zucchini Cake

For all you zucchini lovers out there, here's a luscious cake just for you!

1 cup sugar
2½ cups flour
½ tsp. baking powder
1½ tsp. baking soda
½ tsp. cinnamon
4 tbs. cocoa

½ cup oil
1 cup buttermilk
1 tsp. vanilla
2 eggs
2 cups finely shredded zucchini
4 ozs. mini chocolate chips (optional)

Sift together flour, baking powder, baking soda, spices and cocoa and set aside. In a large mixing bowl beat eggs, sugar, oil, vanilla and buttermilk. Stir in dry ingredients and beat well. Fold in zucchini and mini chips. Pour into a 9" x 13" pan that has been sprayed with nonstick cooking spray. Bake at 325° for 45 minutes or until a cake tester comes out clean.

Nutritional information per serving   Calories 70; Protein grams 2.4; Carbohydrate grams 8.8; Total fat grams 3.3; Saturated fat grams 1; Unsaturated fat grams 2.3; Cholesterol 12 mg; Sodium 25 mg

Fresh Fruit Tartlets (page 54) ▶

Angelfood Cake

This standard low calorie dessert is a snap to make at home.

1 cup unbleached white flour
¼ cup sugar
1¼ cups egg whites (about 10)
1 tsp. cream of tartar

1 tbs. water
¾ cup sugar
2 tsp. vanilla

Sift flour and ¼ cup sugar twice. Set aside. Whip egg whites until foamy. Add cream of tartar and whip to soft peaks. Add water. Slowly add ¾ cup sugar and whip to wet peaks. Don't overwhip. Sift some of the flour mixture over whites. Fold in gently. Sift remaining flour mixture over whites and fold in. Spoon into ungreased 9" tube pan. Cut through batter with knife to break any air pockets. Bake at 325° on lower oven rack for 45 minutes or until top is light brown and springs back when touched.

Nutritional information per serving Calories 108; Protein grams 4; Carbohydrate grams 23; Total fat grams 0; Saturated fat grams 0; Unsaturated fat grams 0; Cholesterol 0 mg; Sodium 42 mg

---

◀ **Fruit Flan (page 60)**

Strawberry Shortcake

Who doesn't like strawberry shortcake? Unfortunately, it's loaded with calories and fat. In this version, we reduced the fat in the cake and used buttermilk for added tenderness. The cream in the topping is replaced with sweetened yogurt.

Cake:

1 cup unbleached white flour
⅓ cup whole wheat pastry flour
2 tsp. baking powder
½ tsp. baking soda

3 tbs. unsalted margarine
1 tbs. honey
¾ cup buttermilk

Combine dry ingredients. Cut in margarine and honey. Stir in buttermilk. Mix only to blend ingredients. Press into a lightly greased 7" pan. Bake at 375° for 15 to 18 minutes. While cake is cooling, prepare strawberries. Cut cake into 8 pieces. Split each piece horizontally in half. Fill with strawberries. Replace top. Spoon more berries over top and add yogurt topping.

Strawberries:
2 cups sliced strawberries
2 tbs. honey

Drizzle honey over berries and let stand 15 minutes.

Yogurt Topping:
1 cup plain lowfat yogurt
1 tbs. honey
1 tsp. vanilla

Nutritional information per serving   Calories 184; Protein grams 5; Carbohydrate grams 29; Total fat grams 5; Saturated fat grams .9; Unsaturated fat grams 4.1; Cholesterol 2 mg; Sodium 33 mg

---

Cherry Bars

Make sure the cherries are well drained before adding them to the batter.

2 cups flour
½ tsp. baking powder
1 tsp. cinnamon
⅓ cup vegetable oil
⅔ cup sugar

1 cup pitted, chopped, unsweetened cherries
¼ cup pecans, chopped (optional)
1 egg
1 tsp. vanilla

Sift flour, baking powder, and cinnamon together in a bowl and set aside. In a large mixing bowl, beat egg and oil together with sugar and vanilla. Add chopped cherries and pecans and mix well. Add the flour mixture and stir just until blended. Spread in a 7" x 11" pan which has been sprayed with nonstick cooking spray. Bake at 350° for 20-25 minutes or until firm to the touch in the center. Cool and cut.

Nutritional information per bar   Calories 75; Protein grams 5.5; Carbohydrate grams 5.8; Total fat grams 3.3; Saturated fat grams .3; Unsaturated fat grams 3; Cholesterol 15.6 mg; Sodium 0 mg

---

Jam Bars

Here is a basic crust that can be topped with any flavor of jam.

Crust:
⅓ cup unsalted margarine
¼ cup sugar
1 egg
¾ cup whole wheat pastry flour
½ cup unbleached white flour
⅔ cup sugarless jam
¼ cup chopped almonds

Cream margarine and sugar until fluffy. Beat in egg. Stir in flours. Press into a lightly greased 8″ x 8″ pan. Spread jam over crust evenly. Sprinkle nuts over jam. Bake at 350° for 22 minutes until firm. Cool before cutting.

Nutritional information per bar Calories 156; Protein grams 1; Carbohydrate grams 27; Total fat grams 5; Saturated fat grams .9; Unsaturated fat grams 4.1; Cholesterol 23 mg; Sodium 6 mg

Graham Crackers

Is it worth making your own graham crackers? It is if you want to avoid saturated fats and excessive sugar.

1 cup unbleached white flour
¾ cup whole wheat pastry flour
½ cup rye flour
½ tsp. baking soda
1 tsp. baking powder
¼ tsp. cinnamon

7 tbs. unsalted margarine
⅓ cup honey
1 tbs. molasses
2 tbs. cold water
1 tsp. vanilla

Combine dry ingredients. Cut in margarine. Combine wet ingredients and add to dry mixture. Blend well. Chill dough 2 hours. Roll out dough ⅛" thick on a surface dusted with rye flour. Cut into squares. Prick all over with a fork. Place on a lightly greased cookie sheet. Bake at 350° for 15 minutes.

Nutritional information per cracker Calories 106; Protein grams 2; Carbohydrate grams 16; Total fat grams 4; Saturated fat grams .6; Unsaturated fat grams 3.4; Cholesterol 0 mg; Sodium 21 mg

---

Watermelon Popsicles

These pops hit the spot on a hot summer day.

watermelon

Puree watermelon in a blender or food processor. Strain to measure 3 cups watermelon juice. Pour into 6 popsicle molds. Freeze until firm.

Nutritional information per popsicle   Calories 50; Protein grams 0; Carbohydrate grams 11; Total fat grams 0; Saturated fat grams 0; Unsaturated fat grams 0; Cholesterol 0 mg; Sodium 3 mg

---

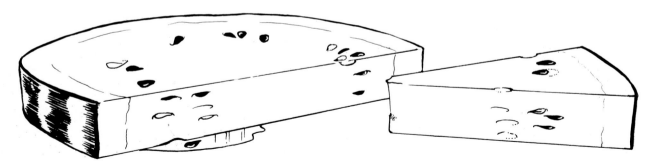

Peachy Pops

This is a fruity popsicle that contains no sugar.

4 fresh peaches
1 cup water
1 tsp. unflavored gelatin
½ cup unsweetened apple juice concentrate, thawed

Place peaches in boiling water for 1 minute to loosen skins. Remove from hot water and place in cold water. When cool enough to handle, peel peaches. Slice and set aside. Soften gelatin in water. Heat over low to dissolve gelatin. Puree peaches, gelatin and apple juice in food processor or blender. Pour into 6 popsicle molds and freeze until firm.

Nutritional information per serving   Calories 53; Protein grams 0; Carbohydrate grams 13; Total fat grams 0; Saturated fat grams 0; Unsaturated fat grams 0; Cholesterol 0 mg; Sodium 0 mg

---

Berry Ice Cream

This really isn't an ice cream because it contains no cream. But this recipe pureed makes such a creamy, fruity ice milk that you'll find yourself calling it ice cream.

3 tbs. cornstarch
1 can (12 ozs.) evaporated whole milk
¼ cup sugar
¼ cup water

1 envelope unflavored gelatin
2 cups pureed berries (strawberries, raspberries or blueberries)
1 cup nonfat dry milk powder

Cook cornstarch, evaporated milk and sugar over medium heat until thickened. Cool. Soften gelatin in water, heating over low heat to dissolve. Place cooked custard, gelatin, berries and dry milk in a food processor or blender and mix until well blended. Place in an ice cream freezer and follow manufacturer's directions. Or, freeze in a shallow pan until slushy. Take from freezer and beat until smooth. Refreeze until ice is solid. Soften slightly at room temperature before serving.

Nutritional information per serving Calories 156; Protein grams 10; Carbohydrate grams 35; Total fat grams 4; Saturated fat grams 2.3; Unsaturated fat grams 1.7; Cholesterol 15 mg; Sodium 135 mg

Blackberry Ice

Substitute any berry for a refreshing frozen ice.

¼ cup apple juice
2 tsp. unflavored gelatin
1½ cups pureed and sieved blackberries
¼ cup honey
1 tsp. lemon juice

Soften gelatin in apple juice, heating over low heat to dissolve. Combine gelatin with remaining ingredients. Freeze until slushy. Take from freezer and beat to break up ice crystals. Refreeze until firm. Let stand at room temperature 10 minutes before serving.

Nutritional information per serving Calories 100; Protein grams 1; Carbohydrate grams 24; Total fat grams 0; Saturated fat grams 0; Unsaturated fat grams 0; Cholesterol 0 mg; Sodium 0 mg

---

Cantaloupe Sherbet

For a melon treat, scoop this sherbet into honeydew melon halves.

2 cups chopped cantaloupe
½ cup skim milk
1 cup orange juice
2 tbs. lemon juice
2 egg whites
¼ cup sugar

In a food processor or blender, puree cantaloupe and skim milk until smooth. Stir in juices and freeze in a shallow pan until firm. Whip egg whites to soft peaks. Slowly add sugar and whip to firm peaks. Take cantaloupe mixture from freezer. Beat until smooth, but not melted. Fold in egg whites. Freeze until firm. Let soften at room temperature 10 minutes before serving.

Nutritional information per serving Calories 80; Protein grams 2; Carbohydrate grams 18; Total fat grams 0; Saturated fat grams 0; Unsaturated fat grams 0; Cholesterol 0 mg; Sodium 33 mg

Peach Sherbet

This sherbet can be made in an ice cream maker. After the yogurt is mixed in, pour it into the ice cream maker canister and follow manufacturer's directions.

3 cups peaches, chopped
1 cup water
¼ cup honey
1 tbs. lemon juice

1 tsp. almond extract
¼ cup apple juice
1 cup plain lowfat yogurt

Cook peaches, water and honey until peaches are soft. Sieve. Stir in lemon juice, almond extract and apple juice. Chill until cool. Whisk yogurt into peach mixture. Pour into an 8" x 8" pan and freeze until ice crystals form around edges, about 45 minutes. Stir crystals into middle of pan and return to freezer. When lightly frozen through, whip mixture until light in color and aerated. Repeat freezing and whipping process again. Spoon into storage container and freeze until firm. Let soften at room temperature 10 minutes before serving.

Nutritional information per serving Calories 84; Protein grams 2; Carbohydrate grams 30; Total fat grams 1; Saturated fat grams .6; Unsaturated fat grams .4; Cholesterol 3 mg; Sodium 20 mg

Creamsicles

Watch these frozen treats disappear before your eyes. Double the recipe and make an even dozen.

⅔ cup nonfat dry milk powder
⅔ cup ice water
6 ozs. unsweetened orange juice concentrate, thawed
1 cup water

Whip dry milk powder with ⅔ cup ice water to soft peaks. Stir in juice concentrate and 1 cup water. Pour into 6 popsicle molds and freeze firm.

Nutritional information per serving   Calories 75; Protein grams 2; Carbohydrate grams 11; Total fat grams 0; Saturated fat grams 0; Unsaturated fat grams 0; Cholesterol 1 mg; Sodium 25 mg

---

Mocha Charlotte

A charlotte usually contains whipped cream and lots of egg yolks. We reduced the amount of yolks and used yogurt instead of cream for a delicious, lowfat charlotte.

1 envelope **plus** 1 tsp. unflavored gelatin
4 tbs. cocoa
⅓ cup **plus** 4 tbs. sugar
⅓ cup strong brewed coffee,
    warm but not hot

1 cup plain lowfat yogurt
½ tsp. vanilla
2 egg yolks
6 egg whites
24 ladyfingers, split lengthwise

In a heavy saucepan, mix gelatin, ⅓ cup sugar, cocoa and egg yolks. Add coffee a little at a time until it is well blended. Cook and stir over medium-low heat until mixture almost boils and gelatin is dissolved. Remove from heat and stir in yogurt and vanilla. Chill until it begins to thicken and just begins to hold its shape.

Beat egg whites until soft peaks form. Add remaining sugar one teaspoon at a time and continue beating until egg whites are glossy and stiff peaks form. Mix about ½ cup of beaten whites into the chocolate mixture, and pour mixture over remaining whites. Gently fold the chocolate into the whites and blend well. Spray bottom and sides of a 9" springform pan with nonstick cooking spray. Line the bottom and sides with ladyfingers. Spoon in ½ chocolate mixture, layer with ladyfingers, and spoon in remaining mixture. Cover with plastic wrap and chill 6 hours or overnight.

Nutritional information per serving   Calories 168; Protein grams 17; Carbohydrate grams 29; Total fat grams 2.2; Saturated fat grams .8; Unsaturated fat grams 1.4; Cholesterol 94 mg; Sodium 83 mg

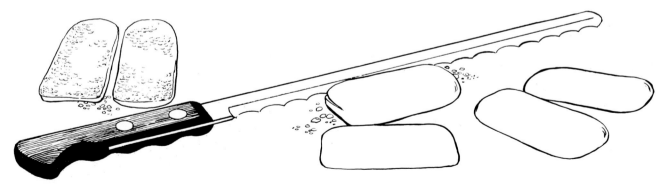

Plum Clafouti

For a nice change of pace, serve this creamy clafouti on a cool summer's evening.

1 lb. ripe plums
1⅓ cups skim milk
2 eggs **plus** 2 egg whites

2 tsp. vanilla
⅔ cup unbleached white flour
⅓ cup sugar

Blanch plums in boiling water for 10 seconds. Peel and slice and set aside. Beat eggs and sugar and then add milk, vanilla and flour and beat well. Spray a 10" pie plate or shallow baking dish with nonstick cooking spray, pour in batter and top with plums. Spread batter over and around plums with the back of a spoon. Bake at 350° for 45 minutes to 1 hour, or until a knife inserted in center comes out clean. Dust with powdered sugar and serve warm.

Nutritional information per serving Calories 140; Protein grams 2.7; Carbohydrate grams 30; Total fat grams 1.5; Saturated fat grams 1.2; Unsaturated fat grams .3; Cholesterol 63 mg; Sodium 50 mg

---

Berry Ice Cream (page 75) ▶

Strawberry Schaum Torte

An easy dessert to make, this combines a crisp, outer shell with a soft center. Fresh strawberries add a fruity touch.

3 egg whites
⅔ cup sugar
1½ tsp. vinegar

½ tsp. baking powder
½ tsp. vanilla
sliced strawberries

Beat egg whites until soft peaks form. Slowly add sugar and continue beating until stiff peaks form. Add vinegar, baking powder and vanilla. Beat until glossy and stiff. Spray a 9" pie plate with nonstick cooking spray. Pile meringue in pan, mounding it in center. Bake one hour at 200°. Cool. Top will fall and crack, leaving a crisp outer crust and a soft mellow center. Serve topped with fresh berries.

Nutritional information per serving Calories 102; Protein grams 1.2; Carbohydrate grams 24.9; Total fat grams 0; Saturated fat grams 0; Unsaturated fat grams 0; Cholesterol 0 mg; Sodium 17.6 mg

◀ Cantaloupe Sherbet (page 77)

Meringue Baskets

There are several steps to this dessert, but the end result will prove that it was worth the effort.

3 egg whites
¼ tsp. cream of tartar
⅔ cup sugar

Beat egg whites and cream of tartar until foamy. Add sugar by tablespoonful and continue beating until meringue is glossy and holds stiff peaks. Be sure not to underbeat. Line a baking sheet with brown paper or baking parchment. Fill a pastry bag with a ½" plain end and pipe meringue into ten 3" circles, building up the sides to form baskets. On another paper lined baking sheet, pipe ten half circles to serve as handles for the baskets. Bake in a 250° oven for 90 minutes. Turn off oven and leave meringues for two more hours. Remove from oven and complete cooling before filling.

Vanilla Cream Filling:

⅓ cup sugar
2 tbs. cornstarch
2 cups skim milk
1 egg **plus** 1 egg white

2 tsp. vanilla
1 drop yellow food coloring (optional)
fresh raspberries for garnish

In a heavy saucepan, mix cornstarch and sugar. Slowly blend in beaten eggs and milk. Cook over medium heat until mixture boils. Continue stirring and boil one minute. Remove from heat and stir in vanilla and food coloring, if desired. Cool with a piece of plastic wrap covering the surface and then chill.

Assembly: Spoon 2 tbs. chilled vanilla cream into each meringue basket. Arrange raspberries on top and tuck in the basket handle. Serve immediately.

Nutritional information per serving Calories 141; Protein grams 3.5; Carbohydrate grams 31; Total fat grams .63; Saturated fat grams, trace; Unsaturated fat grams, trace; Cholesterol 26 mg; Sodium 44 mg

---

Autumn

You know autumn has arrived when the cool weather rekindles your urge to bake. Time to dig out those warm sweaters along with the pungent spices and hearty recipes for fall baking!

You can find a wealth of fall produce in your garden, local orchards and the countryside, as well as at farmers' markets and grocery stores, that would be fun to try in these desserts.

You'll discover a change in these recipes of texture and substance from the lighter summer desserts. Almonds, walnuts, oats and rye all combine with the harvest fruits and vegetables to create a satisfying, nutritious finish to an autumn meal.

Autumn

Peach-Plum Pie

Two of the season's choicest fruits combine to make a peach of a pie.

Crust:
½ cup whole wheat pastry flour
¾ cup unbleached white flour
¼ cup vegetable oil
2-3 tbs. hot water

Combine flours. Stir in oil. Add water slowly and mix until dough balls up. Roll out ¾ of the dough between two sheets of waxed paper. Place in an 8″ pie pan. Reroll the scraps with the remaining dough and cut out various shapes to be placed on top of the filling (perhaps circles or triangles).

Filling:
2 cups peaches (4 medium) peeled and cut in eighths
1½ cups prune plums (10 or 11) cut into fourths
½ tsp. almond extract
3 tbs. unbleached white flour
¼ cup honey

Combine fruits with extract. Toss with flour. Position fruit in the pie crust in a pleasing manner. Drizzle honey over fruit. Place dough cut-outs on top of fruit. Bake at 400° for 25 to 30 minutes until fruit is easily pierced with a knife.

Nutritional information per serving   Calories 190; Protein grams 5; Carbohydrate grams 40; Total fat grams 7; Saturated fat grams .6; Unsaturated fat grams 6.4; Cholesterol 0 mg; Sodium 0 mg

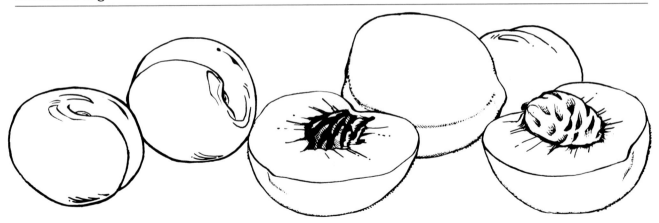

Pumpkin Orange Tart

Citrus orange flavor spices up this tart.

Crust:
½ cup whole wheat pastry flour
½ cup unbleached white flour
3 tbs. unsalted margarine
3-4 tbs. cold water

Combine flours. Cut in margarine. Add only enough water to form a dough. Roll out on a floured piece of waxed paper. Place in a lightly greased 10" flan pan with removable bottom. Prick all over with a fork. Bake at 350° for 12 minutes. Cool slightly before filling.

Filling:
2 cups (16 ozs.) canned pumpkin
⅓ cup sugar
4 egg whites
½ tsp. **each** cinnamon, nutmeg, ginger

½ tbs. unbleached white flour
⅔ cup evaporated skim milk
½ cup orange juice

Combine all the ingredients and beat well. Pour into prepared crust. Bake at 350° for 1 hour. Cool completely before refrigerating or serving.

Nutritional information per serving   Calories 139; Protein grams 4; Carbohydrate grams 25; Total fat grams 4; Saturated fat grams .6; Unsaturated fat grams 3.4; Cholesterol 2 mg; Sodium 29 mg

---

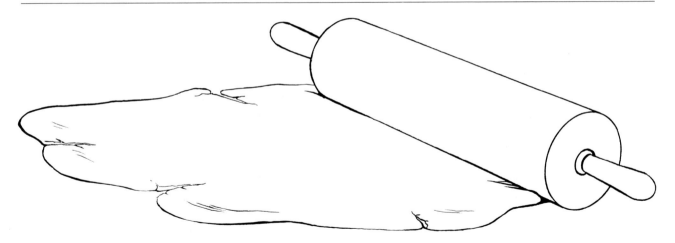

Apple-Pecan Chiffon Pie

Servings: 8

The pecans add a crunch to the smooth texture of the applesauce.

Crust:

½ cup whole wheat pastry flour
½ cup unbleached white flour

3 tbs. unsalted margarine
3 tbs. cold water

Combine flours. Cut in margarine. Add water to form a dough. Roll out on a floured sheet of waxed paper. Place in a 9" pie pan. Prick all over with a fork. Bake at 375° for 12 to 15 minutes until lightly browned. Cool.

Filling:

1 tbs. unflavored gelatin
¼ cup unsweetened apple juice
    concentrate, thawed
1¼ cups unsweetened applesauce
2 tbs. brown sugar

⅛ tsp. cinnamon
2 egg whites, room temperature
⅛ tsp. cream of tartar
2 tbs. sugar
¼ cup finely chopped pecans

Soften gelatin in apple juice concentrate. Heat applesauce, brown sugar and cinnamon. Add gelatin mixture and heat on low to dissolve gelatin. Chill until mixture begins to set, about 1 hour. Whip egg whites until foamy. Add cream of tartar and whip to soft peaks. Slowly add sugar and whip to firm peaks. Fold whites and pecans into applesauce-gelatin mixture. Spoon into prepared pie crust and chill several hours until firm.

Nutritional information per serving   Calories 162; Protein grams 3; Carbohydrate grams 22; Total fat grams 7; Saturated fat grams .7; Unsaturated fat grams 6.3; Cholesterol 0 mg; Sodium 14 mg

Apple Lattice Flan

A centerpiece for the dessert table, this flan has a delectable combination of apples, walnuts and raisins under a lattice crust.

Crust:

1 cup whole wheat pastry flour
¾ cup unbleached white flour
½ tsp. baking powder
⅓ cup oil

5-6 tbs. hot water
1% milk
2 tbs. apple butter

Stir oil into flours and baking powder. Add water slowly until mixture forms a dough. Roll out ¾ of dough between sheets of waxed paper. Place in a 7" x 11" flan pan with removable bottom. Fill with apple mixture and sprinkle with walnuts. Reroll scraps with remaining dough. Cut into 10 strips. Starting at a corner, diagonally place 5 strips evenly across apples. Place remaining 5 strips at right angles to the first strips. Brush strips with milk. Bake at 400° for 35 minutes. While warm, brush with apple butter.

Filling:

3½ cups finely chopped apples (about 3 apples)
½ cup unsweetened applesauce
1 tsp. grated lemon peel
2 tbs. honey

½ tsp. cinnamon
¼ cup raisins
1 tbs. ground walnuts

Combine all except walnuts.

Nutritional information per serving Calories 163; Protein grams 2; Carbohydrate grams 28; Total fat grams 7; Saturated fat grams 1.7; Unsaturated fat grams 6.3; Cholesterol 0 mg; Sodium 17 mg

Pear Almond Tart

This tart blends the mellow flavors of ripe pears and almond custard.

Crust:

⅓ cup whole wheat pastry flour   3 tbs. unsalted margarine
½ cup unbleached white flour   3-4 tbs. cold water

Combine flours. Cut in margarine. Add enough water to hold dough together. Roll out between two sheets of waxed paper. Place in a 10″ flan pan with removable bottom. Prick all over with a fork. Bake at 375° for 8 minutes. Cool.

Almond Custard:

¾ cup milk (1% butterfat)   ½ cup ground almonds
⅓ cup sugar   ¼ tsp. almond extract
2 tbs. cornstarch   2 tsp. vanilla
1 egg, beaten

Cook milk, sugar and cornstarch until thickened. Add egg and cook one minute. Remove from heat and add almonds and extracts. Cool.

Pears:

4 pears, peeled, cored and halved
½ cup unsweetened pineapple juice
  concentrate, thawed
⅓ cup water
2 tsp. lemon juice
2 tbs. sugarless apricot jam

Cook pears in juices and water until tender. Remove pears, setting aside. Cook syrup, reducing to half. Add jam and sieve.

Assembly: Brush hot glaze over shell. Spread almond cream over shell. Slice pears and arrange over cream. Brush pears with remaining glaze. Chill.

Nutritional information per serving Calories 191; Protein grams 3; Carbohydrate grams 31; Total fat grams 6; Saturated fat grams .7; Unsaturated fat grams 5.3; Cholesterol 9 mg; Sodium 19 mg

---

Individual Apple Pies

Beautiful single pies are full of hearty apple flavor.

Crust:
½ cup whole wheat pastry flour
½ cup unbleached white flour
3 tbs. unsalted margarine
3-4 tbs. cold water

Apple Filling:
3 apples, peeled, cored, and thinly sliced
⅓ cup sugarless apricot jam, heated

Combine flours. Cut in margarine. Add only enough water to form a dough. Roll out on a floured piece of waxed paper. Cut out six 4" circles. Place circles on a lightly greased cookie sheet.

Arrange apples in an overlapping pattern on each circle, covering circle completely. Bake at 425° for 20 minutes, or until apples are tender. Spoon melted jam over each pie. Serve warm.

Nutritional information per serving Calories 195; Protein grams 2; Carbohydrate grams 36; Total fat grams 6; Saturated fat grams 1; Unsaturated fat grams 5; Cholesterol 0 mg; Sodium 0 mg

---

Meringue Baskets (page 86) ▶

Plum Strudel

Strudel is a snap to make if you use filo dough. Finely chopped apples can be substituted for the plums.

8 sheets filo dough
2 tbs. unsalted margarine, melted
2 cups small plums, quartered (about 6)

½ cup bread crumbs
3 tbs. sugar

Keep filo sheets covered. Place two filo sheets down on work surface, wide side facing you. Brush lightly with margarine. Repeat using all the filo sheets. Sprinkle top sheet evenly with bread crumbs. Place plums across the top 2". Sprinkle with sugar. Roll up jelly roll style. Seal bottom with margarine. Brush remaining margarine over roll. Prick top all over with a knife. Place on a cookie sheet. Bake at 375° for 25 to 30 minutes until dark golden brown. Serve warm. Or cool and recrisp before serving.

Nutritional information per serving Calories 137; Protein grams 3; Carbohydrate grams 24; Total fat grams 3; Saturated fat grams .4; Unsaturated fat grams 2.6; Cholesterol 0 mg; Sodium 77 mg

◄ Streusel-Topped Pumpkin Oatcakes (page 110)

Filo Fruit Puffs

These flaky pastries are easy to make. Just keep the filo sheets you're not using covered to prevent them from drying out.

Filling:

2 medium apples, peeled,
   cored and finely chopped
¼ cup unsweetened apple juice
   concentrate, thawed

1 tbs. pure maple syrup
⅛ tsp. cinnamon
1 tbs. cornstarch dissolved in 1 tbs. water
3 tbs. raisins

Cook apples, juice, maple syrup and cinnamon over medium heat until apples are just tender. Stir in cornstarch mixture and cook until thickened. Remove from heat and add raisins. Cool.

Puffs:

8 sheets filo dough
1 tbs. unsalted margarine, melted

Work with one filo sheet at a time, keeping others covered. Fold a sheet in thirds lengthwise. Place 2 tsp. filling at the bottom. Fold in the edges ¼" and roll up. Brush all sides including bottom with margarine. Place on a cookie sheet. Repeat with remaining sheets. Bake at 375° for 22 to 25 minutes until golden brown. These are best served warm. Or cool and recrisp in oven when needed.

Nutritional information per serving Calories 113; Protein grams 2; Carbohydrate grams 12; Total fat grams 1; Saturated fat grams .2; Unsaturated fat grams .8; Cholesterol 0 mg; Sodium 72 mg

Pumpkin Cheesecake

This is a rich textured cheesecake with an unexpected flavor — something new to try for Thanksgiving dessert.

Crust:

1¼ cup All Bran or similar cereal
2 tbs. brown sugar

2 tbs. unsalted margarine, melted
1-2 tbs. water

Combine cereal, sugar and margarine. Add only enough water to moisten mixture. Pat into a lightly greased 8″ springform pan. Bake at 375° for 8 to 10 minutes. Cool.

Filling:

2 cups lowfat ricotta cheese
1 egg
3 egg whites
⅔ cup buttermilk
½ cup sugar

¾ cup cooked pumpkin
1 tsp. vanilla
1 tsp. cinnamon
½ tsp. **each** allspice, nutmeg, ginger

Combine ricotta cheese, egg and egg whites in a food processor or blender until smooth. Add remaining ingredients and process until well blended. Pour into prepared crust. Bake at 375° for 50 to 60 minutes. Cool to room temperature. Chill 8 hours or overnight before serving.

Nutritional information per serving   Calories 178; Protein grams 10; Carbohydrate grams 25; Total fat grams 6; Saturated fat grams 1.7; Unsaturated fat grams 4.3; Cholesterol 43 mg; Sodium 140 mg

Apple Cider Carrot Cake

Fresh apple cider is a special autumn treat. It lends a rich, mellow flavor and moistness to the cake.

1½ cups unbleached white flour
½ cup whole wheat flour
3 tbs. wheat germ
2 tsp. baking powder
2 tsp. baking soda
1 tsp. cinnamon
½ tsp. nutmeg
2 eggs
½ cup brown sugar

¼ cup oil
½ cup apple cider
¼ cup plain lowfat yogurt
1 tsp. vanilla
1 tsp. grated orange rind
2 cups grated carrots
1 cup grated apple
⅓ cup raisins

Mix together dry ingredients. Set aside. In another bowl, mix eggs, sugar, oil, cider, yogurt, vanilla and rind. Stir in carrots, apple and raisins. Add to dry ingredients and mix until well blended. Pour into a greased bundt pan. Bake at

350° for 50 to 60 minutes or until toothpick inserted into middle comes out clean. Cool in pan for 30 minutes. Invert onto cake rack. Cool completely.

Nutritional information per serving Calories 157; Protein grams 4; Carbohydrate grams 27; Total fat grams 5; Saturated fat grams .3; Unsaturated fat grams 4.7; Cholesterol 34 mg; Sodium 129 mg

Streusel-Topped Pumpkin Oatcakes

No icing is needed with this sweet streusel topping.

1 cup unbleached white flour
½ cup whole wheat pastry flour
½ cup rolled oats, quick
⅔ cup brown sugar
1 tsp. cinnamon
⅓ cup unsalted margarine

⅔ cup buttermilk
½ tsp. baking soda
2 egg whites
1 tsp. vanilla
½ cup cooked pumpkin

Combine flours, oats, sugar and cinnamon. Cut in margarine until mixture resembles streusel. Reserve ¾ cup. Add remaining ingredients and mix well. Spoon batter into foil cupcake liners. Sprinkle tops with reserved streusel mix. Bake at 350° for 25 minutes.

Nutritional information per cupcake Calories 156; Protein grams 3; Carbohydrate grams 19; Total fat grams 5; Saturated fat grams .8; Unsaturated fat grams 4.2; Cholesterol 0 mg; Sodium 43 mg

Autumn Cranberry Cakes

These little gems are great to serve as after-school treats.

½ cup unbleached white flour
⅓ cup whole wheat pastry flour
½ tsp. baking soda
½ tsp. cinnamon
¼ tsp. cloves
¼ tsp. allspice
¾ cup cranberries, coarsely chopped
  (if frozen, do not thaw before chopping)

2 egg whites
2 tbs. white sugar
¼ cup vegetable oil
½ tsp. vanilla
½ cup rolled oats, quick or regular
¼ cup brown sugar
⅓ cup cranberry juice cocktail
2 tbs. pecans, chopped

Combine flours, baking soda and spices with chopped cranberries. Set aside. Whip egg whites to soft peaks. Gradually add 2 tbs. white sugar and whip to stiff peaks. Set aside. Beat together oil, vanilla, oats and brown sugar. Stir in the flour-cranberry mixture alternately with cranberry juice. Fold in egg whites. Spoon into 12 paper-lined cupcake tins. Sprinkle tops with chopped pecans. Bake at 375° for 18 to 20 minutes.

Nutritional information per cupcake Calories 117; Protein grams 2; Carbohydrate grams 16; Total fat grams 5; Saturated fat grams .8; Unsaturated fat grams 4.2; Cholesterol 0 mg; Sodium 9 mg

Applesauce Bundtlettes

The fancy bundtlette shape makes these cakes a special dessert.

1 cup whole wheat pastry flour
⅓ cup unbleached white flour
¼ tsp. baking soda
¼ tsp. baking powder
½ tsp. cinnamon
⅛ tsp. allspice

2 tbs. honey
2 tbs. oil
2 egg whites
¾ cup unsweetened applesauce
⅓ cup unsweetened apple juice
    concentrate, thawed

Sift dry ingredients. Set aside. Beat honey, oil, egg whites, juice and applesauce together. Add dry ingredients and beat well. Pour into minibundt pans that have been lightly greased. Bake at 350° for 22 to 25 minutes. Cool and ice.

Icing:
2 ozs. neufchatel cheese, room temperature
2 tsp. unsweetened apple juice concentrate, thawed
raisins and almonds to decorate

Beat the cheese and juice until creamy. Spoon over minibundts. Place raisins and almonds on top if desired.

Nutritional information per serving   Calories 195; Protein grams 4; Carbohydrate grams 34; Total fat grams 7; Saturated fat grams .3; Unsaturated fat grams 6.7; Cholesterol 0 mg; Sodium 117 mg

---

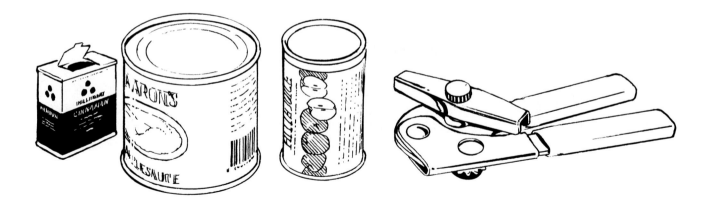

Buttermilk Spice Cake

Servings: 9

Buttermilk makes this cake tender, yet low in fat.

1 cup whole wheat pastry flour
¼ cup unbleached white flour
½ tsp. baking powder
½ tsp. baking soda
1 tsp. cinnamon
½ tsp. cloves
¼ cup vegetable oil

⅓ cup brown sugar
¾ cup buttermilk
½ tsp. vanilla
⅓ cup raisins
2 egg whites
⅛ tsp. cream of tartar
1 tbs. white sugar

whip egg whites (1st in, small, then bowl

Lightly grease a 9″ cake pan. Cut a 9″ circle out of waxed paper and place in pan. Sift flours and spices. Set aside. Combine oil, brown sugar, buttermilk and vanilla. Stir in the flour mixture and raisins. Whip egg whites with cream of tartar to soft peaks. Slowly add sugar and whip to firm peaks. Fold whites into batter. Pour into prepared cake pan. Bake at 350° for 25 to 30 minutes. Cool before glazing.

Glaze:
1 tbs. molasses
1 tbs. sugar
½ tbs. margarine *cook*
2 tbs. powdered sugar *add after cooked*

Bring molasses, sugar and margarine to a boil. Cook 1 minute. Remove from heat and add powdered sugar. Immediately pour over cake, spreading with a spatula. Cool before cutting.

Nutritional information per serving Calories 190; Protein grams 3; Carbohydrate grams 36; Total fat grams 7; Saturated fat grams .5; Unsaturated fat grams 6.5; Cholesterol 0 mg; Sodium 70 mg

Carrot Torte

This carrot torte has the texture of a light spongecake.

4 egg yolks, room temperature
½ cup sugar
⅛ tsp. cinnamon
⅛ tsp. cloves
½ cup unbleached flour
1 tsp. baking powder

1 cup finely grated carrots
1½ cups almonds, ground
1 tbs. rum **or** ¼ tsp. rum extract
4 egg whites, room temperature
¼ cup sugar
powdered sugar

Whip yolks 4 minutes. Gradually add ½ cup sugar, whipping until thick and lemon-colored. Combine flour, spices and baking powder. Carefully stir into yolks. Fold in carrots, almonds and rum. Whip whites to soft peaks. Add ¼ cup sugar slowly, whipping to firm peaks. Fold into yolk mixture. Pour into lightly greased 9" springform pan. Bake at 350° for 40 to 45 minutes. Cool. Remove from pan. Place a paper doily on top of cake. Dust top with powdered sugar. Remove doily.

Nutritional information per serving Calories 160; Protein grams 4; Carbohydrate grams 20; Total fat grams 7; Saturated fat grams .2; Unsaturated fat grams 6.8; Cholesterol 90 mg; Sodium 47 mg

---

Apple Oat Squares

This recipe is also very good with dried fruit mix in place of the apples.

1 cup oats, regular or quick
⅓ cup whole wheat pastry flour
⅓ cup brown sugar
1 tsp. cinnamon
¼ tsp. nutmeg
¼ tsp. baking soda

2 tbs. unsalted margarine, melted
2 tbs. unsweetened apple juice
  concentrate, thawed
1 egg, slightly beaten
1 tsp. vanilla
1 medium apple, finely chopped

Mix the dry ingredients together. Add the remaining ingredients except apples and beat well. Fold in chopped apples. Spread into a lightly greased 11"x 7" pan. Bake at 350° for 25 minutes.

Nutritional information per serving Calories 86; Protein grams 2; Carbohydrate grams 13; Total fat grams 2; Saturated fat grams .4; Unsaturated fat grams 1.6; Cholesterol 23 mg; Sodium 23 mg

---

Gingersnaps

Make these for a welcome addition to lunch boxes.

¼ cup molasses
2 tbs. honey
¼ cup unsalted margarine
¼ tsp. baking soda
1 egg white

¾ cup whole wheat pastry flour
¼ cup **plus** 2 tbs. unbleached white flour
¼ tsp. ginger
⅛ tsp. allspice

Place molasses, honey, margarine and baking soda in a saucepan. Bring to a boil and cook over low heat until mixture foams up. Remove from heat and cool to room temperature. Add remaining ingredients and beat well. Chill dough 2 or more hours. Roll out ⅛" thick. Cut out cookies with a 3" round cutter. Place on a lightly greased cookie sheet. Bake at 350° for 8 to 10 minutes.

Nutritional information per cookie Calories 60; Protein grams 0; Carbohydrate grams 10; Total fat grams 2; Saturated fat grams .1; Unsaturated fat grams 1.9; Cholesterol 0 mg; Sodium 16 mg

Autumn Cranberry Cakes (page 111) ▶

Peanut Butter Cookies

An old favorite is made even more nutritious for you.

½ cup honey
¼ cup vegetable oil
¾ cup peanut butter,
   no sugar added variety
½ tsp. vanilla

2 egg whites
¼ cup nonfat dry milk powder
½ cup whole wheat pastry flour
½ cup rye flour
1 tsp. baking powder

Beat honey, oil, peanut butter, vanilla and whites. Stir in powdered milk. Mix well. Add flours and baking powder. Dough will be very stiff and heavy. Break off pieces and roll into 30 balls. Place on 2 lightly greased cookie sheets. Press a criss-cross pattern on each cookie with a fork, dipping it in water often so it doesn't stick. Bake at 350° for 8 to 10 minutes.

Nutritional information per cookie Calories 87; Protein grams 2; Carbohydrate grams 8; Total fat grams 5; Saturated fat grams .8; Unsaturated fat grams 4.2; Cholesterol 0 mg; Sodium 11 mg

---

◄ Carrot Torte (page 116)

Harvest Moons

A hearty, stick-to-the-ribs cookie just right for crisp autumn afternoons.

½ cup whole wheat pastry flour
½ cup unbleached white flour
½ cup rolled oats, regular or quick
½ tsp. baking soda
½ tsp. cinnamon
⅓ cup brown sugar

⅓ cup granulated sugar
⅓ cup unsalted margarine
½ tsp. vanilla
1 egg white
½ cup cooked pumpkin or squash
  (butternut or hubbard)

Combine flours, oats, baking soda and cinnamon. Set aside. Cream sugars, margarine and vanilla. Add egg white and cream. Stir in pumpkin or squash. Mix in dry ingredients. Drop by teaspoons onto lightly greased cookie sheet. Flatten cookies with wet fingers to ⅛". Bake at 350° for 10 minutes. Cool and ice.

Icing:
6 tbs. sugar
2 tbs. water
2 egg whites

pinch of cream of tartar
½ tsp. vanilla
yellow food coloring

Boil sugar and water to soft ball stage, 238°. Whip whites until foamy, add cream of tartar and whip to soft peaks. Slowly add hot syrup and whip to stiff peaks. Add vanilla and yellow coloring.

Nutritional information per cookie Calories 95; Protein grams 2; Carbohydrate grams 16; Total fat grams 3; Saturated fat grams .5; Unsaturated fat grams 2.5; Cholesterol 0 mg; Sodium 23 mg

---

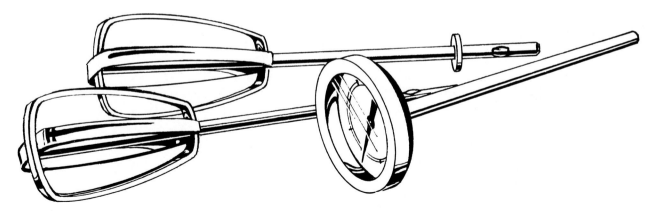

Pumpkin Streusel Bars

You'll be surprised at how fast these delicious bars disappear!

Streusel:
¼ cup unsalted margarine
¼ cup brown sugar
¼ tsp. vanilla

1⅓ cups whole wheat pastry flour
⅛ tsp. cinnamon

Mix ingredients until crumbly. Press ⅔ of mixture into a greased 7" x 11" pan. Bake at 375° about 5 minutes until light golden brown around edges. Cool. Turn oven down to 350°.

Filling:
¼ cup whole wheat pastry flour
¼ tsp. baking powder
⅛ tsp. baking soda
1 egg
1 egg white

¼ cup brown sugar
⅔ cup cooked pumpkin
½ tsp. cinnamon
⅛ tsp. allspice

Combine flour, baking powder and baking soda. Add remaining ingredients and mix well. Spread over crust. Sprinkle remaining streusel over filling. Bake for 20 to 25 minutes until streusel is golden brown.

Nutritional information per bar Calories 190; Protein grams 3; Carbohydrate grams 31; Total fat grams 6; Saturated fat grams 3.5; Unsaturated fat grams 2.5; Cholesterol 30 mg; Sodium 20 mg

Applesauce Cookies

These are soft, sweet cookies with a hint of cinnamon.

1 cup whole wheat pastry flour
1 cup unbleached white flour
1 tsp. baking powder
¼ tsp. baking soda
1 tsp. cinnamon
½ cup vegetable oil

½ cup honey
2 egg whites
½ cup unsweetened applesauce
1 tsp. vanilla
36 whole almonds

Sift dry ingredients and set aside. Combine remaining ingredients except almonds and beat until well blended. Stir in dry ingredients. Drop by teaspoons onto lightly greased cookie sheet. Place an almond in the center of each cookie. Bake at 350° for 8 to 10 minutes.

Nutritional information per cookie Calories 64; Protein grams 0; Carbohydrate grams 8; Total fat grams 3; Saturated fat grams 0; Unsaturated fat grams 3; Cholesterol 0 mg; Sodium 37 mg

Ice Box Cookies

This cookie dough can be kept in the freezer and made up at your convenience.

¼ cup unsalted margarine
⅓ cup honey
1 tsp. vanilla
1 tsp. almond extract
1 egg

1 cup whole wheat pastry flour
½ cup unbleached white flour
½ tsp. baking soda
¾ cup finely chopped almonds

Cream margarine, honey and extracts. Add egg and beat well. Stir in remaining ingredients. Roll dough into a long cylinder 2½" in diameter. Cover and freeze 2 hours. Remove from freezer and immediately slice into 24 cookies. Place on a lightly greased cookie sheet. Bake at 350° for 8 to 10 minutes until golden brown.

Nutritional information per cookie   Calories 70; Protein grams 1; Carbohydrate grams 9; Total fat grams 3; Saturated fat grams .4; Unsaturated fat grams 2.6; Cholesterol 11 mg; Sodium 4 mg

Poached Pears with Brandy Custard

A simple and light dessert to top off a hearty autumn dinner.

Poached Pears

4 pears, peeled, cored and halved
⅓ cup apple-pear juice concentrate
3 tbs. brandy

1 small cinnamon stick
1 tsp. vanilla
2½ cups water

Place all ingredients except pears in a saucepan. Cook over medium heat 5 minutes. Add pears. Cover and simmer 25 minutes until pears are tender, turning pears often. Cool. Refrigerate pears in their liquid 8 hours or overnight.

Brandy Custard:

1 egg, slightly beaten
2 tbs. sugar
1 cup skim milk

2 tsp. cornstarch
1 tbs. brandy

Combine all ingredients except brandy in a saucepan. Cook over medium heat until thickened, stirring constantly. Pour into a bowl, add brandy and stir. Cover with waxed paper and cool to room temperature.

To Serve: Spoon custard into 4 serving dishes. Pears should be at room temperature. Drain pears on paper towels. Place 2 halves in each dish on top of custard. Dust pears with cinnamon or nutmeg.

Nutritional information per serving   Calories 190; Protein grams 7; Carbohydrate grams 37; Total fat grams 1.5; Saturated fat grams .5; Unsaturated fat grams 1; Cholesterol 68 mg; Sodium 50 mg

Fruit Crisp

Try an assortment of fruit for a change of pace.

3 cups peeled sliced fruit
   (apples, pears, peaches, apricots,
   plums or a combination of these)
¼ cup unbleached white flour
¼ cup cornmeal

¼ cup wheat germ
½ cup rolled oats, regular or quick
⅓ cup brown sugar
3 tbs. margarine

Place fruit in a lightly greased 9" x 9" pan. Combine all ingredients except margarine and mix together. Cut in margarine until mixture is crumbly. Sprinkle over fruit. Bake at 375° for 25 to 30 minutes or until fruit is soft and topping is browned. Serve warm with yogurt topping.

Yogurt topping:
2 cups plain lowfat yogurt
⅓ cup sugar

Whisk both together until sugar is dissolved.

Nutritional information per serving Calories 190; Protein grams 4; Carbohydrate grams 27; Total fat grams 5; Saturated fat grams .7; Unsaturated fat grams 4.3; Cholesterol 2 mg; Sodium 70 mg

Caramel Apples

A chewy caramel apple without sugar? Yes! Apple juice concentrate makes a tangy caramel coating that tastes just right with a crisp, juicy apple.

¼ cupmilk (1% butterfat)
½ cup unsweetened apple juice concentrate
½ tsp. vinegar
1½ tsp. unsalted margarine
3 medium apples

Wash apples, remove stems, and stick skewers into stem end of apples. Bring milk and concentrate to a boil. Add vinegar and cook mixture to soft ball stage, 238°. Be careful not to burn it! Take form heat and add margarine. Beat until slightly thickened. Dip apples into candy, turning to coat all sides. Place on waxed paper that has been greased. Cool completely before eating.

Nutritional information per serving Calories 163; Protein grams 0; Carbohydrate grams 36; Total fat grams 2; Saturated fat grams .5; Unsaturated fat grams 1.5; Cholesterol 1 mg; Sodium 19 mg

Pumpkin Parfaits

Spicy pumpkin mousse is layered with a creamy ricotta filling for an elegant dessert.

½ envelope unflavored gelatin
⅓ cup cold water
¼ cup brown sugar
1¼ cup canned pumpkin
⅓ cup water

¼ tsp. ginger
¼ tsp. cinnamon
2 egg whites
⅛ tsp. cream of tartar

Soften gelatin in ⅓ cup water five minutes. Heat brown sugar, pumpkin, ⅓ cup water and spices. Add gelatin and heat to dissolve. Chill mixture until partially set. Whip whites to soft peaks with cream of tartar. Fold into pumpkin mixture. Spoon into 4 parfait glasses alternately with ricotta filling. Refrigerate several hours until set.

Ricotta filling

½ cup lowfat ricotta cheese
¼ cup nonfat dry milk powder
2 tbs. sugar

Combine all ingredients and mix well.

Nutritional information per serving Calories 172; Protein grams 8; Carbohydrate grams 22; Total fat grams 2; Saturated fat grams 1.6; Unsaturated fat grams .4; Cholesterol 11 mg; Sodium 116 mg

Apple Snow with Caramel Sauce

Servings: 4

This luscious caramel sauce can be used on other desserts as well.

Apple Puree:

2 apples
2 tbs. water
1 tsp. vanilla

2 egg whites
2 tbs. sugar

Peel, core and chop apples. Cook in a saucepan with water until very soft. Puree in a food processor or blender with vanilla. Puree should be very thick. Whip egg whites until foamy. Gradually add sugar and whip to firm peaks. Fold whites into apple puree. Spoon into 4 dessert dishes and chill. Drizzle caramel sauce over puree before serving.

Caramel Sauce:

1 tbs. margarine
¼ cup brown sugar

2 tbs. evaporated skim milk
1 tsp. cornstarch

Mix margarine in a saucepan. Add sugar. Cook until sugar is dissolved, stirring constantly. Dissolve cornstarch in milk. Add to sugar mixture. Cook over medium heat until thick, about 1 minute. Sauce will thicken slightly as it cools. Cool completely.

Nutritional information per serving   Calories 157; Protein grams 2; Carbohydrate grams 32; Total fat grams 3; Saturated fat grams .5; Unsaturated fat grams 2.5; Cholesterol 0 mg; Sodium 37 mg

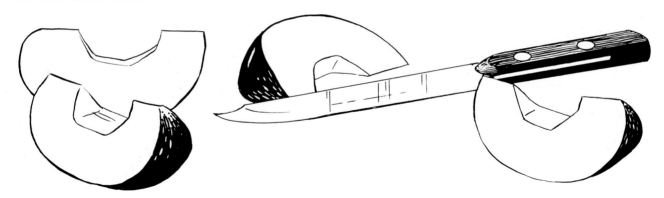

Winter

Winter, that picture post-card image of pristine beauty, exists mainly in our summer dreams. In reality, once the holidays are over, most of us resign ourselves to the cold, dark days ahead.

As cabin fever sets in, it's hard to stay fit and eat properly. With just a little planning and effort, though, you can make tasty, nutritious desserts that fit into a prudent diet.

By getting the whole family involved with baking on weekends, you can have fun together while making quick and easy desserts for the week ahead. Many of these recipes freeze well and make great lunchbox treats.

These desserts are hearty and substantial without being laden with fat and calories. By using bananas, dates, apricots, prunes and other dried fruit, you can cut down the amount of sugar in many recipes, making them naturally sweet, moist and flavorful. Chocolate lovers don't have to forgo the pleasures of rich, chocolatey desserts. You can substitute cocoa, which is much lower in fat than baking chocolate, with no difference in taste. Lowfat dairy products,nuts, and grains combine to boost the nutritional value of these desserts.

Chocolate Yule Log (page 144) ▶

Winter

Baklava

You can make low calorie, low fat baklava. The trick is to brush each sheet very lightly with margarine. The addition of bread crumbs to the filling also reduces the calories.

4 sheets filo dough
½ cup ground walnuts
½ cup toasted bread crumbs

¼ tsp. cinnamon
2 tbs. honey
2 tbs. unsalted margarine, melted

Combine walnuts, bread crumbs, cinnamon and honey. Set aside. Cut the sheets into fourths so you have 16 sheets. Lightly brush a 7" x 11" pan with margarine. Place 8 sheets in pan, one at a time, brushing each lightly with margarine. Spread walnut mixture over the 8th sheet. Top with the remaining sheets, brushing each lightly with margarine. Score the top into 12 pieces. Bake at 375° for 22 minutes until golden brown. Drizzle hot syrup over the top. Cool and cut where baklava is scored.

Syrup:
2 tbs. honey
2 tbs. water
½ tsp. lemon juice

Combine ingredients in a saucepan and bring to a rolling boil.

Nutritional information per serving Calories 104; Protein grams 1; Carbohydrate grams 12; Total fat grams 5; Saturated fat grams .5; Unsaturated fat grams 4.5; Cholesterol 0 mg; Sodium 27 mg

---

Cottage Cheese Pastries

Cottage cheese makes these pastries tender without adding more fat.

Filling:
1 cup blueberries (if frozen, thawed)
¼ cup unsweetened pineapple juice concentrate, thawed
1½ tbs. cornstarch

Bring all ingredients to a boil, stirring. Crush berries. Boil over medium heat until mixture thickens. Cool.

Pastry:
½ cup lowfat cottage cheese
¼ cup vegetable oil
¼ cup sugar
2 tbs. milk (1% butterfat)

½ tsp. vanilla
¾ cup whole wheat pastry flour
¾ cup unbleached white flour
1 tsp. baking powder

In a food processor or blender, blend cheese, oil, sugar, milk and vanilla until smooth. Add flours and baking powder. Knead until dough forms a smooth ball.

Roll out dough ⅛" thick. Using a 3½" cookie cutter, cut out 15 circles (reuse dough scraps). Brush edges of each circle with water. Place a teaspoon of filling in the middle of each circle. Fold circles in half and crimp edges with a fork. Place on a lightly greased cookie sheet. Bake at 375° for 15 minutes or until light brown. Cool.

Nutritional information per pastry   Calories 107; Protein grams 2; Carbohydrate grams 15; Total fat grams 4; Saturated fat grams 2.6; Unsaturated fat grams 1.4; Cholesterol 0 mg; Sodium 31 mg

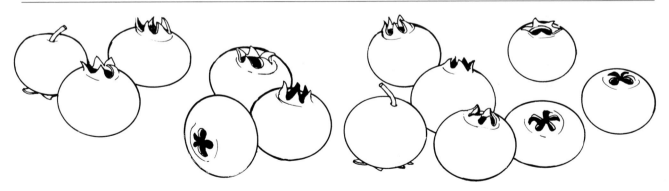

Chocolate Yule Log

Servings: 12

A very festive and delicious cake for the holidays.

Cake:

¾ cup unbleached white flour
¼ cup cocoa
1 tsp. baking powder
2 eggs, room temperature
2 egg whites, room temperature
½ cup sugar

⅓ cup water
1 tsp. vanilla
cranberries coated with egg white and
   rolled in sugar
greens

Sift flour, cocoa and baking powder three times. Set aside. Whip eggs and egg whites for 3 minutes. Add sugar gradually and whip for 3 minutes more. Fold in water and vanilla. Gently fold in flour mixture. Pour into a lightly greased 15" x 10" x 1½" jelly roll pan lined with parchment or waxed paper. Bake at 350° for 12 to 15 minutes. Invert onto a waxed paper-lined towel. Remove paper from bottom of cake. Roll up cake and towel from narrow end. Cool. Unroll and spread filling evenly over cake. Roll up and place on a serving plate, seam side down. Ice to look like a log. Decorate with greens and cranberries.

Filling:

2 egg whites
½ tsp. cream of tartar
¼ cup water

1 envelope unflavored gelatin
½ cup sugar
¼ cup water

Whip egg whites with cream of tartar to soft peaks. Set aside. Soften gelatin in ¼ cup water. Boil sugar and remaining ¼ cup water to soft ball stage, 240°. Take care not to burn syrup! Slowly pour syrup into egg whites. Whip one minute. Add softened gelatin slowly. Whip to firm peaks. Cool slightly before using.

Icing:

1½ cups low fat ricotta cheese
¼ cup sugar
¼ cup cocoa

Mix in a food processor or blender until smooth.

Nutritional information per serving Calories 154; Protein grams 6; Carbohydrate grams 34; Total fat grams 2; Saturated fat grams 6; Unsaturated fat grams 1.4; Cholesterol 50 mg; Sodium 77 mg

---

Prune Cake

Yes! Prunes make a moist, tasty cake. The buttermilk glaze adds just the right sweetness.

2 egg whites
⅓ cup vegetable oil
¾ cup buttermilk
1 tsp. vanilla
⅔ cup brown sugar
1 cup unbleached white flour

½ cup whole wheat pastry flour
½ cup baking soda
½ tsp. cinnamon
½ tsp. nutmeg
1 cup chopped pitted prunes

Beat well egg whites, oil, buttermilk, vanilla and brown sugar. Stir in flours, baking soda and spices. Fold in prunes. Pour into a 7" x 11" lightly greased pan. Bake at 350° for 22 minutes. Let cake cool for 5 minutes. Pierce cake at one inch intervals with toothpick and pour glaze over. Cool before serving.

Glaze:

¼ cup sugar

2 tbs. unsalted margarine

2 tbs. buttermilk

⅛ tsp. baking soda

½ tsp. vanilla

In a saucepan, bring all except vanilla to a boil. Cook over medium heat until mixture becomes golden brown, about 5 minutes. Remove from heat and add vanilla. Immediately spread over warm cake.

Nutritional information per serving Calories 167; Protein grams 2; Carbohydrate grams 29; Total fat grams 6; Saturated fat grams 1.4; Unsaturated fat grams 4.6; Cholesterol 0 mg; Sodium 55 mg

Gingerbread with Lemon Sauce

Servings: 12

The tart lemon sauce brings out the sweetness in the cake.

½ cup buttermilk
⅓ cup brown sugar
¼ cup unsulphured molasses
¼ cup vegetable oil
1 tsp. baking soda

1 egg
¾ cup rye flour
¾ cup unbleached white flour
1 tsp. ginger
½ tsp. cinnamon

Combine all ingredients except flours and spices. Mix well. Add flours and spices and beat two minutes. Pour into a lightly greased 11" x 7" pan. Bake at 350° for 20 minutes. Serve warm with warm sauce.

Lemon Sauce:
¾ cup water
3 tbs. sugar
1½ tbs. cornstarch

¼ cup lemon juice
1 tbs. grated lemon peel

In a saucepan, bring water, sugar and cornstarch to a boil. Cook until thickened, stirring. Remove from heat and add lemon juice and peel.

Nutritional information per serving Calories 150; Protein grams 2; Carbohydrate grams 32; Total fat grams 5; Saturated fat grams .2; Unsaturated fat grams 4.8; Cholesterol 23 mg; Sodium 80 mg

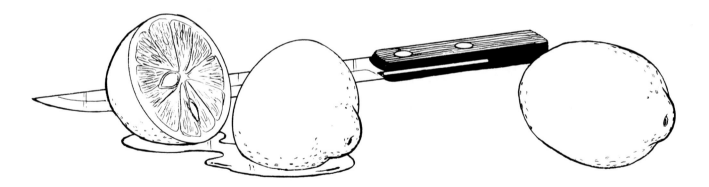

Citrus Spice Sponge Cake

The combination of orange, lemon and spices gives this sponge cake extra flavor.

¾ cup **plus** 2 tbs.
   unbleached white flour
1 tsp. baking powder
⅛ tsp. **each** cloves and allspice
¹⁄₁₆ tsp. nutmeg
3 egg yolks
¼ cup orange juice
⅓ cup sugar

1 tsp. vanilla
1 tbs. grated orange peel
1 tbs. grated lemon peel
7 egg whites
½ tsp. cream of tartar
⅓ cup sugar
1 orange, cut in half and each half sliced
   in fifths, making 10 half slices

Sift flour, spices and baking powder. Set aside. Whip yolks 2 minutes. Dribble in orange juice while whipping. Gradually add sugar and whip 3 more minutes until yolks are thick. Fold in vanilla and grated peels. Whip egg whites until foamy. Add cream of tartar and whip to soft peaks. Gradually add sugar and whip to wet peaks. Fold the flour into the yolk mixture and then fold in the whites, taking care not to deflate. Pour into an ungreased 9" tube pan. Bake in the lower third of oven at 325° for 40 minutes or until cake springs back when touched. Invert pan to cool. When cooled, remove from pan and spoon glaze over cake. Place orange slices on top of cake.

Glaze:

1¼ cups orange juice
¼ cup sugar
2 tbs. cornstarch

2 tsp. grated lemon peel
2 tsp. grated orange peel

Cook juice, sugar and cornstarch until thick. Remove from heat and stir in grated peels. Cool slightly before using.

Nutritional information per serving Calories 156; Protein grams 5; Carbohydrate grams 31; Total fat grams 2; Saturated fat grams .5; Unsaturated fat grams 1.5; Cholesterol 82 mg; Sodium 84 mg

---

Fudgy Cocoa Cakes

Servings: 12

These fudgy cakes are wonderful dusted with a sprinkling of powdered sugar. For a special dessert treat, try the peanut butter frosting.

1 cup unbleached white flour
⅔ cup sugar
1 tsp. baking soda
1 tsp. baking powder
⅓ cup cocoa

1 egg white
⅓ cup hot water
⅓ cup plain lowfat yogurt
1 tsp. vanilla

Sift dry ingredients. Combine remaining ingredients. Add dry ingredients and mix until well blended. Pour into 12 foil-lined cupcake pans. Bake at 350° for 18 minutes. Cool before frosting.

Peanut Butter Frosting:

1 cup powdered sugar
¼ tsp. vanilla

2 tbs. unsweetened peanut butter
4 tbs. nonfat dry milk powder

Combine all ingredients and cream well.

Nutritional information per unfrosted cake Calories 99; Protein grams 2; Carbohydrate grams 24; Total fat grams .5; Saturated fat grams .4; Unsaturated fat grams .1; Cholesterol 0 mg; Sodium 122 mg

Carob Cake

No, carob is not chocolate, but this cake proves that carob can make as moist and wonderful a cake as the richest chocolate can.

1 cup whole wheat pastry flour
6 tbs. carob flour
1 tsp. baking soda
¼ cup vegetable oil
⅓ cup honey
1 egg

1 egg white
1 tsp. vanilla
¼ tsp. almond extract
¾ cup buttermilk
⅓ cup sugarless jam
powdered sugar

Sift flour, carob and baking soda. Set aside. Combine remaining ingredients except jam and powdered sugar and mix well. Stir in flour mixture and beat one minute. Pour into an 8″ cake pan that has been lightly greased. Bake at 350° for 22 to 25 minutes. Cool. Split cake in half horizontally. Spread jam over bottom layer. Replace top layer. Place a doily on cake top. Sprinkle with powdered sugar. Remove doily.

Nutritional information per serving Calories 184; Protein grams 3; Carbohydrate grams 30; Total fat grams 7; Saturated fat grams .5; Unsaturated fat grams 6.5; Cholesterol 0 mg; Sodium 110 mg

Banana Bars

Use the very ripest bananas for the best flavor.

½ cup whole wheat pastry flour
½ cup unbleached white flour
½ tsp. baking soda
½ tsp. baking powder
1 egg
1 egg white

½ cup sugar
1 tsp. vanilla
¼ cup unsalted margarine, melted
2 medium bananas, mashed
⅓ cup plain lowfat yogurt

Sift flours, baking soda and baking powder. Set aside. Beat egg, egg white and sugar for 2 minutes. Add bananas and melted margarine. Stir in flour mixture alternately with yogurt. Pour into a lightly greased 11" x 7" pan. Bake at 350° for 22 to 25 minutes or until done.

Nutritional information per serving Calories 108; Protein grams 2; Carbohydrate grams 15; Total fat grams 4; Saturated fat grams .7; Unsaturated fat grams 3.3; Cholesterol 18 mg; Sodium 60 mg

**Orange-Glazed Carrot Currant Bars (page 162) left,
Strawberry Teacakes (page 33) top,
Brownies (page 168) right, Cut-out Cookies (page 160) bottom ▶**

Molasses Cookies

These soft, plump cookies are full of rich molasses flavor.

¼ cup vegetable oil
¼ cup honey
⅓ cup molasses
½ tsp. baking soda
3 tbs. warm water

1 cup whole wheat pastry flour
1 cup unbleached white flour
1 tsp. ginger
¼ tsp. **each** allspice and nutmeg

Beat oil, honey, molasses and baking soda together. Add remaining dry ingredients and stir to combine. Chill dough several hours (or ½ hour in the freezer). Divide dough into 18 pieces. Place the pieces on a lightly greased cookie sheet. Flatten with wetted fingers to ⅛". Bake at 350° for 10 minutes.

Nutritional information per cookie Calories 93; Protein grams 2; Carbohydrate grams 16; Total fat grams 3; Saturated fat grams .8; Unsaturated fat grams 2.2; Cholesterol 0 mg; Sodium 23 mg

Date Delights

For apricot delights, substitute dried apricots for the dates.

1⅓ cups quick oats
⅓ cup brown sugar
¼ cup whole wheat pastry flour
¼ cup unbleached white flour

3 tbs. unsalted margarine
1½ tbs. unsweetened apple juice
  concentrate

Combine oats, brown sugar and flours. Cut in margarine. Toss mixture lightly with apple juice concentrate, taking care not to overmix. Press ⅔ of mixture firmly into a lightly greased 8" x 8" pan. Spread evenly with date filling. Sprinkle remaining mixture over filling. Press lightly. Bake at 350° for 20 minutes.

Filling:
1 cup chopped dates
¼ cup orange juice
¼ cup water

Place dates, juice and water in a saucepan. Cook over medium heat until dates are very soft and liquid is absorbed. Cool before using.

Nutritional information per serving Calories 155; Protein grams 3; Carbohydrate grams 29; Total fat grams 4; Saturated fat grams 2.5; Unsaturated fat grams 1.5; Cholesterol 0 mg; Sodium 0 mg

Cut-Out Cookies

A versatile dough, this can be cut out into many shapes.

⅓ cup vegetable oil
½ cup sugar
2 egg whites
1 tsp. lemon juice

1 tsp. vanilla
1½ cups unbleached flour
1 tsp. baking powder

Combine oil and sugar. Add whites one at a time, and then lemon juice and vanilla. Mix flour, powder and nutmeg. Add to mixture. Chill dough in freezer for 10 minutes. Roll out ⅛" thick. Cut out cookies with a 3" round cookie cutter. Bake at 350° for 7 to 10 minutes. Cool and decorate.

Icing:
1 egg white
¼ tsp. cream of tartar
2 tbs. honey

1 tsp. vanilla
1 cup nonfat dry milk powder

Beat egg white with cream of tartar until frothy. Beat in honey and vanilla, and then dry milk.

Nutritional information per cookie   Calories 75; Protein grams 3; Carbohydrate grams 13; Total fat grams 3; Saturated fat grams .2; Unsaturated fat grams 2.8; Cholesterol 1 mg; Sodium 68 mg

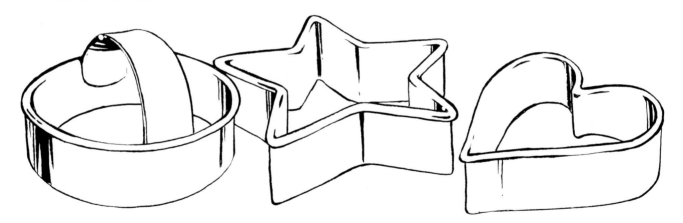

Orange-Glazed Carrot Currant Bars

Servings: 20

Carrots make these bars deliciously moist.

1¼ cups unbleached white flour
1 cup whole wheat pastry flour
1 tsp. ginger
½ tsp. baking powder
½ cup sugar
½ cup vegetable oil

2 egg whites
1 tsp. vanilla
1 tbs. grated orange peel
1½ cups grated carrots
¼ cup currants

Combine flours, baking powder and ginger. Set aside. Mix sugar, oil, egg whites and vanilla until well blended. Stir in carrots and currants. Add dry ingredients and mix just to blend in. Pour into a lightly greased 9" x 13" pan. Bake at 350° for 20 to 25 minutes. Glaze bars while still warm.

Glaze:
⅔ cup powdered sugar
1½ tbs. unsweetened orange juice concentrate, thawed

Beat sugar and juice together until smooth.

Nutritional information per serving   Calories 153; Protein grams 2; Carbohydrate grams 24; Total fat grams 6; Saturated fat grams .1; Unsaturated fat grams 5.9; Cholesterol 14 mg; Sodium 19 mg

Lebkuchen (Honey Bars)

Servings: 12

This is our version of the traditional honey bars. Instead of candied fruit, we use lemon and orange peels to give a citrus flavor without the added calories.

6 tbs. honey
¼ cup sugar
½ tbs. grated lemon peel
½ tbs. grated orange peel
½ tsp. allspice
¼ tsp. cinnamon
1 egg white
2 tbs. skim milk

½ cup whole wheat pastry flour
½ cup unbleached white flour
¼ tsp. baking soda
¼ cup ground almonds
¼ cup chopped dried fruit
   (dates, apricots or apples)
skim milk

Heat honey and sugar to dissolve sugar. Remove from heat, pour into a bowl and beat in peels, spices, egg white and milk. Stir in flours and baking soda. Beat well. Stir in almonds and dried fruit. Spread into a lightly greased 11" x 7" pan. Brush top with milk. Bake at 350° for 22 minutes or until middle springs back when touched. Don't overbake. Glaze bars while still warm.

Glaze:

2 tbs. honey
2 tbs. water

Bring honey and water to a boil. Cook over medium heat for 1 minute. Pour hot glaze over warm bars.

Nutritional information per serving   Calories 105; Protein grams 2; Carbohydrate grams 24; Total fat grams 1; Saturated fat grams 0; Unsaturated fat grams 1; Cholesterol 0 mg; Sodium 6 mg

Spice Cookies (Spekulatius)

These special cookies are a treat for the holidays. If you don't have the wooden mold, the cookies still taste great cut out in any shape.

1½ cups unbleached white flour
1 cup whole wheat pastry flour
½ cup sugar
1½ tsp. baking powder
½ tsp. cinnamon

½ tsp. carob or cocoa
⅛ tsp. cloves
¼ cup unsalted margarine
2 egg whites
¼ cup milk (1% butterfat)

Combine dry ingredients. Cut in margarine. Stir in egg white and milk. Mix to form a dough. Roll out dough to ¼" thickness. Cut out cookies with a 3" cookie cutter. Or press dough into a well-floured wooden Spekulatius mold, cut away excess dough and flip cookie out onto a lightly greased cookie sheet. Bake at 350° for 8 to 10 minutes.

Nutritional information per cookie Calories 66; Protein grams 2; Carbohydrate grams 11; Total fat grams 2; Saturated fat grams .3; Unsaturated fat grams 1.7; Cholesterol 0 mg; Sodium 26 mg

---

Meringue Kisses

You can change the taste and flavor of these light, airy cookies by substituting your favorite dried fruit.

3 egg whites
⅔ cup sugar
¼ tsp. cream of tartar

½ cup sugarless flake cereal
¼ cup chopped dates
¼ cup chopped walnuts

Whip egg whites, sugar and cream of tartar to firm peaks in a double boiler set over simmering water, about 5 minutes. Remove from heat and fold in cereal, dates and walnuts. Drop by teaspoon onto a cookie sheet lined with parchment paper or aluminum foil. Bake at 325° for 30 minutes. If not completely dry to the touch, turn oven off and let cookies sit in oven for 15 minutes. Cool completely before storing.

Nutritional information per cookie Calories 25; Protein grams 0; Carbohydrate grams 5; Total fat grams .5; Saturated fat grams 0; Unsaturated fat grams .5; Cholesterol 0 mg; Sodium 6 mg

Brownies

When you want a rich, fudgy treat, this is it!

½ cup brown sugar
2 tbs. cocoa
3 tbs. unsalted margarine, melted
1 egg, beaten
1 tsp. vanilla
½ cup unbleached white flour
powdered sugar

Sift together brown sugar and cocoa. Beat in melted margarine, egg and vanilla. Stir in flour. Pour into an 8" x 8" lightly greased pan. Bake at 325° for 22 to 25 minutes. Don't overbake! Cool and dust with powdered sugar.

Nutritional information per serving Calories 92; Protein grams 0; Carbohydrate grams 13; Total fat grams 4; Saturated fat grams .2; Unsaturated fat grams 3.8; Cholesterol 23 mg; Sodium 6 mg

Maple Nut Creams

Ee sure to keep these creams frozen until serving time.

3 ozs. neufchatel cheese
½ cup nonfat milk powder
2 tbs. maple syrup
3 tbs. chopped walnuts

Combine cheese, milk and syrup. Form into 8 balls. Roll in walnuts. Freeze until firm.

Nutritional information per serving   Calories 83; Protein grams 1; Carbohydrate grams 3; Total fat grams 4; Saturated fat grams 1.4; Unsaturated fat grams 2.6; Cholesterol 9 mg; Sodium 88 mg

---

Mocha Cream Hearts

Servings: 4

You don't have to wait for Valentine's Day to make these. Shape the meringues into circles instead of hearts and serve this special dessert often.

Meringue Hearts:
2 egg whites, room temperature
⅛ tsp. cream of tartar
½ cup sugar

Whip whites until foamy. Add cream of tartar and whip to soft peaks. Gradually add sugar and whip to firm peaks. Draw four 4" hearts on a sheet of parchment paper with a dark pencil. Place parchment paper on a cookie sheet, drawing side down. Spoon meringue onto paper following the outlined heart shapes. Build up edges. Bake at 250° for 1 hour. Turn oven off and leave meringues in oven for another hour. Cool completely before filling. Do not refrigerate, as meringues can absorb moisture and crumble.

Custard:

1 cup skim milk
2 tbs. sugar
1 tbs. cocoa
1 tbs. cornstarch

2 tsp. instant coffee powder
1 egg, slightly beaten
1 tsp. vanilla
candied violets

Combine all ingredients except vanilla in a saucepan. Bring to a boil. Cook over medium heat, stirring constantly, until mixture thickens. Remove from heat and add vanilla. Cool. Stir occasionally to prevent skin from forming. Just before serving, spoon custard into meringue hearts. Decorate with candied violets.

Nutritional information per serving Calories 179; Protein grams 5; Carbohydrate grams 38; Total fat grams 1.5; Saturated fat grams .5; Unsaturated fat grams 1; Cholesterol 68 mg; Sodium 74 mg

---

Meringue-Topped Apricot Pudding

This is an unusual way to serve a good pudding.

4 slices whole wheat bread, cubed
2 cups skim milk
1 egg, slightly beaten
1 egg white

1 tsp. vanilla
½ tsp. cinnamon
¼ cup raisins
⅓ cup sugarless apricot jam

Lightly grease an 8" x 8" baking dish. Place bread in the dish. Combine remaining ingredients except jam and pour over bread. Let stand 10 minutes to absorb liquid. Put the baking dish in a pan of hot water. Bake at 350° for 45 minutes or until a knife inserted in the center comes out clean. Remove the baking dish from the pan of hot water. Over low heat, melt jam and drizzle over pudding. Spread meringue over pudding and bake at 350° for 10 minutes or until meringue is browned.

Meringue:

2 egg whites
¼ tsp. cream of tartar
2 tbs. sugar
½ tsp. vanilla

Whip egg whites until foamy. Add cream of tartar and whip to soft peaks. Gradually add sugar and whip to stiff peaks. Fold in vanilla.

Nutritional information per serving Calories 164; Protein grams 7; Carbohydrate grams 32; Total fat grams 2; Saturated fat grams .3; Unsaturated fat grams 1.7; Cholesterol 47 mg; Sodium 183 mg

Chocolate Pudding with
Brown Sugar Meringue

This meringue doesn't have to be baked because it is made with a cooked syrup. If you like the crunch of a baked meringue, spoon the pudding into oven-proof dishes, top with meringue and bake at 350° until meringue is lightly browned.

Pudding:

¼ cup cocoa
¼ cup sugar
2 tbs. cornstarch

2 cups skim milk
1 egg, slightly beaten
1 tsp. vanilla

Combine all ingredients except vanilla in a saucepan. Cook over medium heat until mixture thickens, stirring constantly. Remove from heat and add vanilla. Pour into 5 serving dishes. Cover with meringue and chill before serving.

Meringue:

3 tbs. brown sugar
1 tbs. water

1 egg white, room temperature
⅛ tsp. cream of tartar

Combine brown sugar and water in a saucepan. Bring to a boil and boil one minute. Don't burn! Whip egg white and cream of tartar to soft peaks. Slowly pour in sugar syrup and whip to firm peaks.

Nutritional information per serving Calories 150; Protein grams 6; Carbohydrate grams 27; Total fat grams 2; Saturated fat grams 1; Unsaturated fat grams 1; Cholesterol 56 mg; Sodium 75 mg

---

Caramel Crunchies

Try these sugarless candies next time you crave something sweet.

1 cup unsweetened apple juice concentrate, thawed
1 tsp. vinegar
4 tbs. almond butter or peanut butter
½ cup sugarless flake cereal

Cook juice and vinegar to 238° or soft ball stage. Remove from heat. Add almond butter and cereal. Stir until mixture thickens. Drop 12 teaspoonfuls onto a lightly greased cookie sheet. While still warm but not hardened, form each candy into a square. Chill until firm.

Nutritional information per candy   Calories 65; Protein grams 1; Carbohydrate grams 8; Total fat grams 3; Saturated fat grams 0; Unsaturated fat grams 3; Cholesterol 0 mg; Sodium 6 mg

Banana Apricot Mousse

Apricots lend a lovely peach color and a sweet contrast to the tangy yogurt.

2 medium bananas
½ cup dried apricots
1 cup plain lowfat yogurt
1 tsp. vanilla

Puree all ingredients in a food processor or blender until smooth. Spoon into 4 dessert dishes. Chill well before serving.

Nutritional information per serving Calories 130; Protein grams 4; Carbohydrate grams 28; Total fat grams 1; Saturated fat grams .6; Unsaturated fat grams .4; Cholesterol 3 mg; Sodium 42 mg

---

Adapting Recipes

You don't have to give away your beautiful dessert cookbooks or replace your family's favorite treats with "diet" desserts. It is easy to convert almost any recipe to a slimmed-down version that will look and taste every bit as good and, in same cases, even better.

By using some clever substitutions for fat- and calorie-laden ingredients and by making use of some of the new "lite" products on the market, you can transform almost any glamorous dessert into a delicious low fat treat. Once you learn, it will not be long before you find yourself automatically making these substitutions whenever you pull out one of your old standbys or find a tempting new recipe to try.

With each trip to the market, we discover yet another new product designed to help cut fat and cholesterol out of our diets. The saturated fat in margarine, cream cheese, ricotta and yogurt has been cut or eliminated altogether. There are powdered or frozen egg substitutes with little or no fat or cholesterol. Many cooking oils are available with no cholesterol. Some are in the form of convenient nonstick cooking sprays which add practically no calories and are great for keeping food from sticking to baking pans.

Don't despair if your recipe calls for heavy cream. Evaporated skim milk or plain yogurt with a little added sugar will do the trick. If the cream is to be beaten, substitute two or three egg whites with a tablespoon of sugar for each white and beat them until they hold stiff peaks. The meringue can then be folded into the recipe just like whipped cream. The addition of a small amount of plain gelatin will help a whipped, chilled dessert hold its shape.

Butter in recipes adds a great deal of saturated fat and cholesterol which can be eliminated by using margarine. If you wish to reduce fat further, use the "diet" margarines which are one-third to one-half water. The unsalted margarines also help eliminate unneeded sodium. Many recipes will actually be improved in texture and taste by cutting the amount of fat called for. For a moist texture in recipes that call for one cup of oil, butter or margarine, use half the amount and replace the rest with yogurt or buttermilk.

Baking chocolate is another source of saturated fat and cholesterol. A rich chocolate taste can be achieved by substituting powdered cocoa. Three tablespoons of cocoa contain 45 calories and 2.7 grams of fat. The equivalent amount, one ounce of solid baking chocolate, is 141 calories and contains 14.8 grams of saturated fat.

Cheesecakes and other cream cheese or sour cream based desserts can be made with wonderful results. Low fat or skim milk ricotta in combination with buttermilk or yogurt gives excellent results. Cream cheese can also be replaced with the new "lite" varieties or with yogurt cheese made by draining plain yogurt in a cheesecloth bag overnight. In recipes calling for sour cream, use instead, low fat cottage cheese with a bit of yogurt or lemon juice blended in a food processor until it is creamy.

Egg substitutes can be used interchangeably with whole eggs; just follow the guidelines on the carton. These products eliminate all the fat and cholesterol and are made mostly from egg whites. If you do not wish to use these products, you can get great results simply by using one whole egg and replacing the rest of the eggs called for with egg whites. Some recipes will work just as well without any egg yolk.

You will find it fun to experiment and you may even come up with some inventive substitutions of your own. The following are a few examples of how much of the fat, cholesterol and calories can be eliminated from some basic recipes.

Chocolate Pudding, Version 1

Servings: 4

½ cup sugar
2 tbs. cornstarch
2 cups whole milk
2 egg yolks

1 tbs. butter
2 ozs. semi-sweet baking chocolate
2 tsp. vanilla

Nutritional information per serving   Calories 321; Total fat grams 36; Saturated fat grams 13.2; Unsaturated fat grams 22.8; Cholesterol 157 mg; Sodium 149 mg

Chocolate Pudding, Version 2

Servings: 4

⅓ cup sugar
2 tbs. cornstarch
2 cups skim milk

1 egg
4 tbs. cocoa
2 tbs. vanilla

Nutritional information per serving   Calories 171; Total fat grams 2.3; Saturated fat grams .5; Unsaturated fat grams 1.8; Cholesterol 51 mg; Sodium 55 mg

Pumpkin Pie, Version 1

Servings: 8

Pastry for 10" pie:

1⅓ cups flour
½ tsp. salt

½ cup lard
3-4 tbs. cold water

Pumpkin Custard Filling:

3 eggs
2¾ cups cooked pumpkin
1 cup sugar
1 tsp. salt
1½ tsp. cinnamon

¾ tsp. ginger
½ tsp. nutmeg
½ tsp. cloves
2¼ cups cream

Nutritional information per serving   Calories 535; Total fat grams 36.8; Saturated fat grams 15; Unsaturated fat grams 21.8; Cholesterol 151.7 mg; Sodium 412 mg

---

Pumpkin Pie, Version 2

Pastry for 10″ pie:

1¾ cups flour

5 tbs. unsalted margarine

3-4 tbs. cold water

Pumpkin Custard Filling:

1 egg **plus** 2 whites **or**
    egg substitute to equal 3 eggs

2¾ cups cooked pumpkin

⅔ cup sugar

1½ tsp. cinnamon

¾ tsp. ginger

½ tsp. nutmeg

½ tsp. cloves

2¼ cups evaporated skim milk **or**
    ½ skim milk and ½ evaporated skim milk

Nutritional information per serving Calories 267; Total fat grams 7.9; Saturated fat grams 3.1; Unsaturated fat grams 4.8; Cholesterol 32.6 mg; Sodium 98.5 mg

Basic Plain Layer Cake, Version 1

Servings: 12

2 cups flour
1½ cups sugar
3½ tsp. baking powder
1 tsp. salt

½ cup butter
1 cup whole milk
1 tsp. vanilla
3 eggs

Nutritional information per serving   Calories 266; Total fat grams 10.4; Saturated fat grams 5.2; Unsaturated fat grams 5.2; Cholesterol 88.6 mg; Sodium 187 mg

---

Basic Plain Layer Cake, Version 2

Servings: 12

1⅓ cups flour
2 tsp. baking powder
½ tsp. baking soda
⅔ cup sugar
¼ cup vegetable oil

2 tsp. vanilla
1 cup buttermilk
3 egg whites
¼ tsp. cream of tartar

Nutritional information per serving   Calories 140; Total fat grams 4.5; Saturated fat grams .3; Unsaturated fat grams 4.2; Cholesterol .83 mg; Sodium 38.4 mg

---

Index

Angelfood cake, 67
Apple
  cider carrot cake,
    108
  lattice flan, 96
  oat squares, 117
  snow with caramel
    sauce, 134
  pecan chiffon pie, 94
  pies, individual, 100
Applesauce
  bundtlettes, 112
  cookies, 126
Autumn cranberry
  cakes, 111

Baklava, 140
Banana(s)
  apricot mousse, 177
  bars, 154
  orange tart, 10
  flambé, 43
  in pastry, 15
Berry ice cream, 75
Blackberry ice, 76
Brownies, 168

Buttermilk spice cake,
  114

Cake(s)
  about, 7
  angelfood, 67
  apple cider carrot,
    108
  applesauce
    bundtlettes, 112
  autumn cranberry,
    111
  basic plain layer
    cake, version 1,
    184
  basic plain layer
    cake, version 2,
    184
  basic white, 28
  buttermilk spice, 114
  carob, 153
  carrot torte, 116
  chocolate yule log,
    144
  chocolate zucchini,
    64

Cake(s) (cont.)
  citrus spice sponge,
    150
  cocoa chiffon, 62
  decorated party, 31
  eggplant, 61
  fudgy cocoa cakes,
    152
  gingerbread with
    lemon sauce, 148
  maple chiffon, 24
  pineapple-filled, 23
  prune, 146
  pumpkin
    cheesecake, 106
  rhubarb, 22
  strawberry
    shortcake, 68
  streusel-topped
    pumpkin oatcakes,
    110
Cantaloupe sherbet, 77
Caramel
  apples, 131
  crunchies, 176
Carob cake, 153

Carrot
  torte, 116
  currant bars, orange
    glazed, 162
Cheesecake
  farina, 26
  pumpkin, 106
Cherry
  bars, 70
  pie, fresh, 58
Chocolate
  pudding with brown
    sugar meringue,
    174
  yule log, 144
  zucchini cake, 64
Citrus spice sponge
  cake, 150
Cocoa
  chiffon cake, 62
  cakes, fudgy, 152
Cookies
  about, 7
  applesauce, 126
  banana bars, 154
  brownies, 168

METRIC CONVERSION CHART

Liquid or Dry Measuring Cup (based on an 8 ounce cup)
1/4 cup = 60 ml
1/3 cup = 80 ml
1/2 cup = 125 ml
3/4 cup = 190 ml
1 cup = 250 ml
2 cups = 500 ml

Liquid or Dry Measuring Cup (based on a 10 ounce cup)
1/4 cup = 80 ml
1/3 cup = 100 ml
1/2 cup = 150 ml
3/4 cup = 230 ml
1 cup = 300 ml
2 cups = 600 ml

Liquid or Dry Teaspoon and Tablespoon
1/4 tsp. = 1.5 ml
1/2 tsp. = 3 ml
1 tsp. = 5 ml
3 tsp. = 1 tbs. = 15 ml

Temperatures

°F		°C
200	=	100
250	=	120
275	=	140
300	=	150
325	=	160
350	=	180
375	=	190
400	=	200
425	=	220
450	=	230
475	=	240
500	=	260
550	=	280

Pan Sizes (1 inch = 25mm)
8-inch pan (round or square) = 200 mm x 200 mm
9-inch pan (round or square) = 225 mm x 225 mm
9 x 5 x 3-inch loaf pan = 225 mm x 125 mm x 75 mm
1/4 inch thickness = 5 mm
1/8 inch thickness = 2.5 mm

Pressure Cooker
100 Kpa = 15 pounds per square inch
70 Kpa = 10 pounds per square inch
35 Kpa = 5 pounds per square inch

Mass
1 ounce = 30 g
4 ounces = 1/4 pound = 125 g
8 ounces = 1/2 pounds = 250 g
16 ounces = 1 pound = 500 g
2 pounds = 1 kg

Key (America uses an 8 ounce cup — Britain uses a 10 ounce cup)

ml = milliliter
l = liter
g = gram
K = Kilo (one thousand)
mm = millimeter
m = mill (a thousandth)
°F = degrees Fahrenheit

°C = degrees Celsius
tsp. = teaspoon
tbs. = tablespoon
Kpa = (pounds pressure per square inch)
    This configuration is used for pressure cookers only.

Metric equivalents are rounded to conform to existing metric measuring utensils.